Nevertheless

PEACE IN SPITE OF PAIN

SHARONDA JONES

Little Phoenixes Publishing
Upper Marlboro, Maryland

Little PHOENIXES Publishing

Nevertheless

Copyright © 2017 by Sharonda Jones

All rights reserved. No part of this publication may be reproduced, distributed or transmitted in any form or by any means, including photocopying, recording, or other electronic or mechanical methods, without the prior written permission of the publisher. Send permission and ordering requests to:

Little Phoenixes Publishing
PO Box 7281, Upper Marlboro, Maryland 20792
www.littlephoenixes.com

Publishers Cataloging-in-Publication Data

Name: Jones, Sharonda, author.
Title: Nevertheless : peace in spite of pain / Sharonda Jones.
Description: Upper Marlboro, MD : Little Phoenixes, 2017.
Identifiers: LCCN 2017949985 | ISBN 978-0-999-2380-0-4 (pbk.) | ISBN 978-0-9992380-1-1 (hardcover) | ISBN 978-0-9992380-2-8 (ebook)
Subjects: LCSH: Adult child sexual abuse victims— Biography. | Child sexual abuse. | Life change events. | Self-help techniques. | Spiritual life. | Adjustment (Psychology) | BISAC: BIOGRAPHY & AUTOBIOGRAPHY / Personal Memoirs. | BIOGRAPHY & AUTOBIOGRAPHY / Women. | SELF-HELP / Abuse. SELF-HELP / Spiritual.
Classification: LCC HV6570.2 .J66 2017 (print) | LCC HV6570.2 (ebook) | DDC 362.76092--dc23.

Unless otherwise indicated, all Scripture quotations are from the New King James Version of the Bible. Copyright © 1982 by Thomas Nelson, Inc. Used by Permission.

Cover design: Maceo Jones
Book Layout ©2017 BookDesignTemplates.com
Printed in the United States of America

*This book is dedicated to my Lord and Savior,
Jesus Christ, for giving me
strength and grace to overcome.*

*To my husband, for loving, pushing, providing, and
allowing me to be all that God has put in me to be.
I am forever yours.*

*To my gifts, for the joy it gives me to be your mom.
I dream, believe, and rise so that
you will go bigger, be bolder, and shine
brighter than your hearts can imagine.*

To my mom, all that I am, I give in honor of you.

Acknowledgments

This book would not be a reality without the help and encouragement of many amazing people. I am blessed to have such a tremendous amount of love and equally I pray you all know my heart toward you.

Eloise Dillard, Barbara Pyndell and family – I love you all a bushel and a peck, and a hug around the neck. Thank you for being part of my village.

Elijah and Marilyn Thorne – God gave me you. Thank you for being my dad on earth and another mom to love me through this life.

Maceo Jones – you are my best decision. I give you my life. I will never be able to fully wrap my mind around how, why, or what it takes to love me and yet you do, every single day. Your love has helped me to grow into the woman I am and I will forever love, cherish and honor you for your love and support.

Vinincia Dorsey – my confidant, my sister, my friend. Thank you for being true. I will love you always.

Charlyne McWilliams – thank you for being the first eyes for my book, my encourager and, of course, my Victory sister.

Kingdom Knights Motorcycle Ministry – thank you for supporting 'Sista Phoenix' and all my "missions". When I need you, you are there and that means the world to me.

Drs. Mike and Dee Dee Freeman – thank you for being my godly examples in the earth. I've learned from your lifestyle and your teachings, and have grown in my faith to see the manifestations of the promises of God.

Contents

Introduction ix

Part One – DREAM

Chapter One..1

Chapter Two...15

Chapter Three..29

Chapter Four..43

Chapter Five...63

Chapter Six...79

Chapter Seven... 101

Chapter Eight.. 117

Part Two – BELIEVE

Chapter Nine... 133

Chapter Ten... 155

Chapter Eleven.. 175

Chapter Twelve 199

Part Three – RISE

Chapter Thirteen 219

Chapter Fourteen 235

Chapter Fifteen 257

Chapter Sixteen 275

Prayer of Salvation 289

Introduction

Have you ever experienced paralyzing anxiety or been so overwhelmed by a fear of the unknown that it kept you from enjoying life's simple pleasures? Perhaps you know someone whose obsession with worrying causes them to create a false wall of protection, and when moments of joy do appear, they take every measure to avoid them.

If you answered no, then allow me to introduce myself, my name is Sharonda and I did everything in my power to sabotage anything that might represent happiness. I would fight seeing the glass full, half full or even with a drop of water in it at all to avoid any chances of hopefulness. When my stress became more than I could handle, I would go to the most isolated room, pick a corner and shrink myself as much as possible. Holding my knees to my chest, my focus only on controlling my breathing and not losing my mind. My attacks, which I decided came as a result of a lapse in my ability to limit moments of joy, would cause an overwhelming sensation of suffocation. I hated feeling this way and yet I was clueless as to how to prevent those moment from returning. Consistent in my life were deep periods of depression from which I felt only death could free me.

Life was hard and I accepted the reality of a hard life as an unavoidable fate. My mom had a hard life and her mom had a hard life, therefore I expected the same for me as well as for my children. Who was I to desire any differently?

Sabotage: *deliberately destroying something of value*. This was my solution to controlling what happened to me and how it happened. When I found myself enjoying an encounter, I ended it. When I began to succeed at a task, I found fault and decided I had to start over. While most people shun away from starting over, the ability to drop everything and begin again was passed down to me from my mom as if it was eye color or hair texture DNA. As much as I needed love, peace, and joy, I never expected to experience them as long as pain was present. And I concluded that it always would be. As my hated of life grew, so did depression, diminished self-worth, and the desire to be isolated from others. Whenever there was a period of happiness, I prepared myself for the letdown that was sure to follow.

Eventually I learned I could desire more and that I could have better. I learned despite the pain we experience in the natural, God has provided for us a rock, a foundation and a source of strength that can carry and sustain us through the journey called LIFE. God has given to every believer the promise of peace in spite of pain; joy and happiness are ours if only we surrender all to Him.

Fear is a tool of Satan to destroy our lives, our future and our hope. Leaning more to our own understanding rather than the Word of God and the direction of Holy Spirit perpetuates this fear. From fear, a downward spiral begins and is impossible to break free from without faith in the One who came to give us abundant life. Without a relationship with Jesus Christ through Holy Spirit, one will never fully understand the depth of God's unfailing love and the fulfilment of the peace that overcomes fears.

> *"The thief does not come except to steal, and to kill, and to destroy. I have come that they may have life, and that they may have it more abundantly."*
>
> John 10:10

As a child, I was raised worshipping gods and deities through sacrificial offerings and ceremonious rituals reminiscent of the practices of my African ancestors. There were different gods for the different elements of nature, who required the shed blood of animals to hear my prayers, free me from burdens or bless my life. Revelation of God's love through His Begotten Son was a gift that I received later in life and since then, I've grown and continue to grow in understanding of who I am according to God's Holy Word. I now walk boldly in the fullness of the peace that God's Word provides. It is the journey of how I once crawled and stumbled before learning to walk in this boldness that I gladly share with you today.

NEVERTHELESS

This book is divided into three parts: **Dream, Believe** and **Rise.**

In Dream, I share the early periods of my life in which I had no control over how my life was being shaped; it was as if I was asleep and dreaming. We moved around more than I can remember; I attended six different elementary schools and still to this day have trouble recalling where I lived and when. People came and went in my life during this time, some making lasting effects and others I can barely remember their names.

In the second part, Believe, I share coming to know Jesus and how the truest love changed my life. I learned to appreciate my desire to laugh. I gained wisdom and understanding through periods of wilderness moments. I began to see *believing* requires operating in a belief if I ever wanted to see it come to pass. I surrendered a tremendous amount of myself for the pursuit of love, peace and happiness but I didn't realize I was only creating a fallacious place of peace that would unravel with little effort. When I stopped looking for love, I found it. When I stopped sabotaging moments in my life that were filled with love, I was able to experience them fully with expectation of peace. When I stopped trying to be accepted, I realized I already possess the only acceptance that matters, God's.

It wasn't until I learned who I am in Christ that I began to rise, which is the third section, and overcome those things which Jesus took upon the Cross on my behalf. In Rise, I bring you to the present day and show you how important it is to continue to grow in faith as you follow Christ.

My hope is that the words written on these pages will inspire you and remind you of the awesome glory of God, as well as encourage you to look over your own "through-story" to recognize the same love that God has showered over you. My desire is that you'll see God as a God of 'nevertheless', one of more than enough, always faithful and forever loving.

I warn you in advance that some of what you will read may shock you, anger you, and perhaps even offend you but please know that everything written here is for the single purpose of victory. Satan wanted me dead and at one point in my life, so did I. But God had other plans for me just like He has for you.

NEVERTHELESS

For I know the thoughts that I think toward you, says the Lord, thoughts of peace, and not of evil, to give you a future and a hope.

Jeremiah 29:11

Regardless of the situation, God says to keep our eyes fixed on Him. Regardless of how the circumstances look, God says no weapons formed against us shall prosper. Regardless of how much we've done that we think disqualifies us from the promises of God, His Word says "Nevertheless" and shows us grace and mercy from destruction in the wilderness. What an awesome God we have!

Therefore, I pray sharing my journey blesses you along your own personal journey THROUGH. I pray you receive revelation of God's love, the strengthening of your faith and the manifestation of your victory, in the name of Jesus.

Love always,

Sharonda

SHARONDA JONES

DREAM

> *"There is no greater agony
> than bearing an untold
> story inside you."*
>
> –MAYA ANGELOU

1

Although the death, burial and resurrection, along with my acceptance of Jesus Christ as Lord, guarantees me victory over sin, the enemy was determined to take me out of the game and off the court before I could become a member of the Body of Christ team. The spirit of death has zealously pursued me and sought my destruction since the first moment air filled my infant lungs on the early morning of Sept. 24, 1975.

Like a slave owner riding the toughest stag in his stable, led by the meanest pack of dogs on the hunt for a runaway slave in the middle of the night, the enemy has come for me. His goal: to shackle me with the chains of pain and the bondage of anxiety. Out of fear, I ran as if my life depended on it. I kept running, not sure where I was headed but certain that nothing good would come from me stopping.

Clumsily, I stumbled my way through the thick vegetation and darkness of life, searching for a place to hide and people to confide, listening for sounds of peace and protection. When life had calmed, or at least felt like it had, I would exhale to welcome a freedom like that which my ancestors who fled slavery in the South prayed they would experience once they reached the North. But soon I would discover the chase did not cease, it just slowed for the bend in the road or had taken on a different direction.

Admittedly, there were times in my life during the chase when I wanted to surrender, I tried to surrender, threw my hands up, dropped to my knees and waited for darkness to overtake me.

"Surely death couldn't be as bad as this life was proving to be," I thought to myself.

But I lived. My heart continued to pump blood through my veins and my chest continued to rise and fall with every breath, all for a greater purpose that I would one day realize.

In reflection, it makes sense why I felt chased. When I was five years old, my mom pulled off a movie style escape scene, similar to Jennifer Lopez's character in the movie *Enough*. With two bags packed, one for her and a smaller case for me, she waited until the late-night hours to escape from an abusive relationship. Rather than seeing it as a triumph for my mom, I resented deserting my childhood home and the only place where I had a sense of happiness, love, family and security. By her urgency, it was clear we were running from something or someone but the specifics were not to be shared with her young child. My place was to do as I was told. I turned to look out of the rear window and watched what was once my life, fade away as the distance grew between us. It had to have been terrible, right? It had to be something so very horrible to cause my mom to leave all my clothes that wouldn't fit in my one suitcase, all my toys, all my memories behind in that house. I trusted her and chose to believe where we were headed had to be better than where we left. It wasn't.

SHARONDA JONES

Born in Charlotte and for the first five years, I was raised as a Christian. My mom read the Bible, we celebrated Christmas, and I loved getting dressed up for Easter. Though our family was small, I had friends who were as close to me as blood-relatives. That is until the night we left without a single word, and from that night, everything changed for me. The secrets that were once hidden from me and the pain my mom endured began to manifest in my life. My mom chose to no longer be a follower of Christ and instead began following the religious beliefs of the people who opened the doors of their homes to us when we had nowhere else to go.

Insecure and unsure of who I was or where to place my trust caused me to become weary of all the things I didn't understand, which led me to withdraw into myself. I hated not knowing my future or where we were going to live. Not knowing why any of it was happening or how to deal with it all. The void from the lack of emotional stability and guidance left me longing for what was missing, looking for what would sustain me in people rather than in my Creator.

My mom trusted the people who took us in. I'm not sure if it was because they deserved it or if it was

NEVERTHELESS

because she had no choice. Unfortunately, her trust was taken advantage of on many occasions and we suffered financially, physically and emotionally as a result.

> *Sever yourselves from such a man, whose breath is in his nostrils; for of what account is he?*
>
> Isaiah 2:22

My mom believes she was born in 1949, in Mecklenburg County in Charlotte, North Carolina. The reason Charlotte is presumably her birthplace is because she has no official proof of her birth. She has conducted vital record searches and found mentions of a baby girl Lewis born on her birthdate but the person listed as the mother is not the person who raised her. She concluded she was a home birth, born to a young unwed girl and raised by a family relative, which was common for poor blacks living in the South during that time. What is more of a mystery to me is how she was able to go through life without a legal birth certificate, enroll in school and work her first job when today, since 9/11, a person can barely purchase a pair of socks without a retina scan.

SHARONDA JONES

The first set of official records my mom ever received was from her marriage to Eddie Watts at the age of 18. She would joke it was a shotgun wedding with the shotgun pointed on her. From that marriage, she gave birth to two sons, Charles in 1968 and Eddie Jr. in 1969. Both boys passed away before their first birthdays. I couldn't imagine losing a child, least alone two.

Since pregnancy was the reason she married Eddie, after the death of her second son, Eddie, Jr., she left the marriage for a life on her own, though never legally divorcing him. Five years later, she gave birth to her first and only daughter, me. I always wondered how my mom must have gotten through that first year of my life, having gone through the experience of losing two children and not sure if death of her child would happen for a third time.

As for how I came to be, my mom enjoys sharing what she considers a love story of sorts. I don't necessarily agree. One evening while enjoying herself at a local bar, in walked a military serviceman, fair-skinned, average height with "good hair". She said he was a marine on leave and out for the evening. She proudly recalls that she *knew* at that exact moment he would be my father because the "spirits told her so" implying direction came from a celestial higher being. I always teased her and said, "You must mean the spirits of the Jack Daniels persuasion?"

My next response to this part of the story, once I grew old enough to not get backhanded in the mouth, was "too bad the spirits didn't tell you to get a social security number."

My mother and father connected soon after that meeting and just as she had predicted, or better yet planned, she became pregnant with me. Initially, he didn't take her seriously when she shared the news they would have a child together, he must have thought she was crazy or, more likely, was used to women making those types of claims. Either way, I'm sure he enjoyed the conception process along the way.

Following the news of her pregnancy, he wasn't in the picture long enough to know that he now had a daughter in the world.

With her previous loss, I assumed my second birthday would be reason enough to celebrate, confirming my mom's hopes and putting to bed any fears that motherhood was not for her. However, I don't think she saw it that way. Into my adulthood my mom still mourned for them, and I don't fault her for her grief. I wish I could have known my big brothers, been a little sister to them and a recipient of their love, protection, and guidance. I used to wonder how differently my life would have been if they were a part of it, whether my mom would have been so sad all the time, and would I have spent so many years feeling lonely and lost. I imagined a family that consisted of more than two people. I wondered if she would have had the ability to care for three children when, at times, raising one child seemed overwhelming.

From some of the stories my mom has told me over the years, I know it wasn't easy for her to raise a child alone, having not dealt with or healed from the grief of losing two children, a failed marriage, and the abandonment of the Marine who left her to raise her child fatherless. I realize there were many mistakes made along the way, but now that I'm a mom, I have a greater understanding of the responsibility that rested on her shoulders. When I look back over my life, having come to terms with the consequences that came along with her decisions, I am reminded that she didn't have to keep me. She could have left me by the roadside, she could have allowed so much more to happen to me. But she didn't. She tried to protect me the best she knew how, and although her protection wasn't enough to keep hurt and danger from me, she persevered and that makes her one of the strongest women I know.

Though the lessons she taught me about love probably weren't the ones she meant to teach me, I gained valuable insight about love; what love is and what love isn't based on her quest to attain it. The expression "more is caught than taught" pretty much summed up my childhood, with the added notion that children should be seen and not heard. I saw a lot, said little and mostly used my imagination to fill in the rest. I'll just say this was a recipe for many, many mistakes to be made along the way.

The pain she carried from her childhood into her adult life was transferred to me like energy that moves from one object to another. I was the child she was supposed to love and protect; I longed for her to cover me but the reality was what I longed for from her, she longed for too.

SHARONDA JONES

Most of my time as a child was spent alone which was intentional. My goal was to stay out of my mom's way and to limit the stress on her as much as possible, which I hoped would make her happy. As a result, I withdrew more and more into myself. It seemed to please her that I didn't require much attention. The only problem was that I was desperately in need of it.

Looking back over how I spent my days, I can see the early signs of withdrawal and the triggers that should have been addressed:

When I heard...	*I felt...*
"Go outside and find someone to play with." →	Deserted and left alone.
"She's a loner, that's just the way she is." →	Unsure how to interact with others.
"She's got an attitude problem. That's why she doesn't talk." →	Insecure and unsure how to communicate it.
"I'm doing the best I can. Don't be ungrateful." →	Guilty for wanting her love, affection, and attention.

NEVERTHELESS

Withdrawal and isolation are tools of a guileful enemy, used to distract us from our purpose and the promise of peace for our lives. It is much like the divide and conquer approach used in war. This is where the enemy begins to separate us from God and from His love, but since He can't remove God's love for us, he attacks our thoughts and plants seeds of doubt to convince us that we are unworthy of it. Doubt becomes insecurity and insecurity becomes disparagement. The pain that was unresolved in my mom's life now formed in me as weeds stealing away the sustenance that allowed me to grow spiritually. If left untreated and not uprooted, the pain of my mom's life would one day attempt to block me from the life filled with the peace, happiness and joy that I desperately sought.

Slowly, the vibrancy of what I was to become was draining from me and I was powerless in my youth to stop it. Although during this period of my life my mom had denounced Christianity and was practicing a different belief, I felt a covering over me from when we once honored Jesus as Lord, except I was too young to understand exactly what it was.

Perhaps you have experienced this or something similar in your life. Ever wondered why God kept you through the storms before you accepted Jesus as Lord? The answer is simple, because He loves you and wants you to know it. There's a call on your life, a testimony in your heart that can be used not only to glorify Him but to reclaim from the enemy that which belongs to you, such as your peace and your joy. God sent Jesus to save the world for one reason, and that reason is love.

> *For God so loved the world, that he gave his only begotten Son, that whosoever believeth in him should not perish, but have everlasting life. For God sent not his Son into the world to condemn the world; but that the world through him might be saved.*
>
> John 3:16-17
>
> *But God demonstrates His own love toward us, in that while we were still sinners, Christ died for us.*
>
> Roman 5:8

He showers us with His love and mercy even when we live like we don't deserve it and even when

NEVERTHELESS

everything around us seems to be in complete and utter chaos. His love is still with us even when we are in the wilderness of confusion. When we are not looking to Him or don't even know how to seek Him, God has His hand stretched out toward us ready to steady us when we stumble. We don't have to 'find' love because love is not lost. We simply must receive it, by faith, through Jesus.

It would be more than ten years before I did just that.

SHARONDA JONES

A picture of me as a little girl in
Charlotte, North Carolina

2

Everything important in my life seems to have occurred in threes, which is astonishingly appropriate considering three is the number of divine perfection. In addition to Holy Trinity, the number three can be found in other areas of our existence such as:

> ***Universe*** – *consists of time, space and matter.*
> ***Man*** – *is a spirit, with a soul and living in a body.*
> ***Bear Witness in the Earth*** – *the Spirit, the water and the blood.*

Three is also present in the number of children I have, times I've been married (though one man I married twice), and the number of legal identities I've claimed (more on this later). Then there's love.

Love can be viewed in three ways: God's love, love of self and love for others. In Dr. Dave Martin's book, *The 12 Traits of the Greats*, he teaches that the three ways to view love are from the perspective of others, our own perspective, and God's view of us. Most of my life I've based my self-image and worth on others' perspective of me, those over my care, and those whose care I wished to be under.

In the dictionary, love is defined simply as an emotion. But to a born-again believer, love is so much more. God is love, God created love, God gave love and God has assigned us to love others. Besides, what other three words have as much power as the words *I love you*? Even the sting from the words "I hate you" can be healed and forgiven by words of love. The word "love" possesses great power. This is the principle in which we were created, to love. We were made for love, in the image of love and for the exchange of it.

We are born with an innate desire to be attached to and provided for by another, but as we mature and

NEVERTHELESS

develop, that attachment and dependency should diminish. Sadly, there are many who associate the dependency on affection from others with love when love is not intended to be based on what is received.

Love is about the opposite; love is about giving to the betterment of another person without the desire for anything in return. Love is patient, long suffering, does not envy, not vain, never fails and covers a multitude of sin. *(1 Cor. 13:4-8)*

Before we left Charlotte, N.C., and before my mom decided she would no longer follow Christ, we lived a simple life filled with all the rewards of loving one another. Those times were wonderful; I will forever be grateful and cherish them. From the few celebrations of Christmas and Easter, to reading the Bible and saying our prayers before retiring at night, I believe it was those early moments in my life that helped to frame some of the life-altering decisions I would later make in adulthood. It was established in me that joy and faith in Jesus went together, hand in hand, and connected us to God's love.

We lived in a 900 s.f. 2-bedroom, 1-bathroom house, on the corner of Seigle Avenue and East 16th

Street, in the Belmont area of Charlotte. It had just enough room for my mom and me, but as a child I thought it was huge. On the front porch, my mom kept all her plants. Her acclaimed green thumb, capable of bringing plants on the verge of death back to a life of beauty and splendor, was not passed down to her only daughter.

The porch sat high enough off the street to create a perfect perch for a princess to look out over her land and survey it whenever her heart desired. As was common in the 1970s, my neighborhood was an extension of our yard and home. Down the street to the left of our house was my babysitter and the kids in the neighborhood were my playmates. Everyone knew everyone, which really meant everyone knew everyone else's business.

In our small kitchen, I loved helping her cook, especially my favorite foods like homemade buttermilk biscuits and collard greens. My role in making biscuits was to roll out the dough with the rolling-pin and to use the rim of a cup as a cutter to separate the dough into perfect round beauties. Butter and honey were the only accompaniments for our biscuits. Jelly was for P&J sandwiches only. My

NEVERTHELESS

mom was a master at preparing turkey necks and greens, macaroni and even liver, though I refused to eat liver. To me it was horribly disgusting. I'll never understand the fascination with liver, or chitterlings but I'm getting off the point.

We lacked the material things that everyone else seemed to have. In fact, we were the family that received the donated dinners from churches and schools, free bread, peanut butter and cheese from distribution centers, clothes that friends had gotten their full use of, and of course the monthly financial support from the government, otherwise known as welfare. If it was not included in the dinner boxes, on the list of allowed purchases from Women Infants and Children (WIC), or within the budget of our food stamp allotment, then we went without it. Though this may all sound unfortunate to some, the reality and the blessing is that our needs were met. My mom made sure we had what we needed; there was no desire for what I didn't know I lacked. My mom and I took evening walks; she made up stories that soloed me as the princess; we cooked together and enjoyed being a family of two. No other home, city or time that followed our departure from Charlotte ever compared to this time in my childhood. I felt loved and secure.

I learned to master a posture of grateful humility and to appreciate everything that was given to us. As a high school dropout, single parent, with no family support, and receiving government assistance, every day was a struggle that she attempted to keep hidden from others. She raised me to the best of her limited natural and educational ability.

My mom's live-in boyfriend, John, was a tall heavy-set light skinned man with thick black wavy hair. On Fridays, John would come home early from work with a bag of Big Chew bubble gum that I anxiously awaited. Watching the adults, I pretended the gum was snuff and would pack my jaws or lower lip with the sugary strings. When I could no longer resist the sweet syrup filling my mouth, I succumbed to the urge to chew and then repeated the process over again and again until the bag was empty. We would then spend the remainder of the afternoon watching cartoons and soap operas, specifically *Guiding Light* and *As the World Turns*, while I rested my head on the large mound that was belly. Life was simple and expected. I had consistency.

NEVERTHELESS

John worked as a bricklayer and everyday his clothes were filled with construction dust and dirt. My job was to plop down on the floor at his feet, untie his boots and remove them. Dramatically, I would always fall over as I pulled his boots from his feet. Next, his socks. My mom would be in the kitchen preparing dinner. After I had removed his shoes and socks, I went directly to my next job, his hair. It's no wonder why today I have a knack for doing hair and a passion for being a handi-woman around the house.

During the week my activities included hours of play, visiting neighbors if my mom had errands, or helping my mom around the house. On special nights, my mom would hang a large white sheet on the doorway between the living room and dining room and show movies using a reel to reel projector. The picture quality of the movies was always poor but the time spent together was special. I purely enjoyed being next to her, eating stove popped popcorn and drinking soda pop.

After dinner or after watching a movie, I had a chore that I loved to do which was washing dishes. I am not certain of my efficiency with this task, but I don't think my mom had high expectations. She would pull a step stool up to the sink, fill the basin with water and hand me the dish cloth. Somehow it seemed I never had enough detergent at the start and consequently would need to add more, much more. More bubbles, less water, and dishes no longer visible under the mountain of suds was my approach to tackling dirty dishes. I must have been successful because my mom always allowed me to wash them. Even to this day, I much more prefer to wash my dishes by hand though possibly because that's one way I can stay connected to a happier time in my past. Life was good.

But this was my perspective.

Life is not just about what we can see and neither should what we see be our focus. In those years, my mom did her best to protect me from her pain. In fact, she did so well in hiding what she was enduring that I was shocked later when I learned why we left. While my memories of Charlotte were idyllic, my mom's memories of the same time were not. What I thought were trips to the neighbors' homes for friendly visits or babysitting were visits of necessity

NEVERTHELESS

because we had no food in the house or to avoid me being present when she and John fought. When we told stories by candlelight, it was because the electricity was off. When we packed our bags in the middle of the night, it was to avoid the pending eviction that was scheduled to happen the next day and the abuse from John when he found out.

I will never fully know what my mom endured during my younger years and I will always love her for giving it her best. The obstacles she had to overcome, the challenges she faced because of her level of education, and the chains of emotional bondage from the abuse she suffered had to have been tremendous. Yet, she provided for me in spite of her own personal challenges.

Later in my life, her love wasn't enough to protect me from the thoughts that left me vulnerable and susceptible to the attacks of the enemy, but no human love can. We sometimes think and wish the love of a person could protect us, keep us, and provide for us. Only God's love can do this. Becoming familiar with pain can create in a person the lack of comfort in the absence of it. Growing up, I began to connect pain to relationships. I used pain as a reference for situations and circumstances in my life. If there was no pain involved, then it was strange and unsuitable.

As parents, we have the responsibility of planning for our children's future and making decisions that would ultimately affect the rest of their lives. But when a person is struggling with their own fears and pain, their role as a parent falls to a secondary priority. Regardless of what's missing in our lives, we must be true to what is love and what is infatuation masquerading as love. To end perpetual pain and sever the grip of a fallacious infatuation, we must be willing to recognize the two and then address them accordingly.

Fallacious infatuation, or false love, is tool of deception used by the enemy and can be easily identified when there's an accompanying sense of "falling" into it. When we love, there's no sense of falling as if it were a mistake or an unstable footing. Love is intentional; it is God's anticipatory remedy to what troubles us. When we fall, there's an associated expectation for the possibility of getting hurt or experiencing an unpleasant sensation, a sensation that signals our body and our lives that a change is required. Pain can also be the result of something that has nothing to do with a fall or anything external. When there's something inside of you that is in distress, your body gives you notice that attention or adaption is required. This is not always negative.

Look at the butterfly. At a point in the caterpillar's life, it recognizes that the time has come for it to mature. It creates a cocoon for itself and, understanding this is just a temporary state, accepts the unavoidable uncomfortable experience in order to reach maturity. If it never goes through the stress of metamorphosis, it will never grow into the beautiful adult version of itself. If any part of this process is interrupted, the butterfly's ability to function, develop or reproduce as intended will be in jeopardy. The same is true with our lives. The enemy wants to interrupt our development and spiritual growth, he does not want us to reproduce God-loving, faith-filled, followers of Christ. The enemy was pleased with himself when my mom renounced Christianity; he continued to relish as I fell victim to the abuse of others just as my mom did in her youth.

But God didn't allow my story to end there just as yours didn't end after trial, tribulation, lost loves, hurt and abuse. So much is done in the name of love but as believers, we must remember:

- God is love.
- Love from others is not the primary source for love in our lives.
- Love of God is first. Learning to love ourselves and others follows.
- Love forgives.
- Love sustains.

When we choose to love as God intends, we forfeit our way of loving but also, simultaneously hold God accountable for our protection. Honoring God and submitting to His will and purpose puts us securely in and under His cover.

And we have known and believed the love that God has for us. God is love, and he who abides in love abides in God, and God in him.

There is no fear in love; but perfect love casts out fear, because fear involves

NEVERTHELESS

> *torment. But he who fears has not been made perfect in love.*
>
> 1 John 4:16, 18

I often try to imagine had these principles been taught to me throughout my childhood, would I have made some of the same decisions. Would I have had so many challenges with anxiety, loneliness, depression, and low self-esteem? Would I have walked in the confusion of who I was as a person? I journeyed through those years with no clue about God's love for me, or the redemptive grace through Christ that we have access to by faith.

Each day I grew to hate life more and more; yet to my chagrin, I hoped for love. I yearned for acceptance and affection. I dreamed of the day someone would love me in the natural enough to deliver me from the pain that I had become dreadfully accustomed. I hoped for more but I wasn't sure why. I wanted more but I didn't know what. I didn't realize I continued to hope because I was made to have hope. I desired more because God created me for greatness.

3rd grade school picture

3

As a young child, I remember my mom reading Psalm 23 to me. It was my favorite scripture and even after she chose to follow another belief, I held on to the words of who the Lord IS. Hearing those words consoled my spirit even though I was too young to really understand what they meant. My mom was unknowingly planting seeds in my spirit, seeds that would one day grow and blossom into the fruit I would need to sustain me through the trials of life. We didn't know what was waiting for us down the road but God did. His Spirit directed her and I am better because of her blind obedience. With each reading of the scripture, God's Word was building up my strength to make it THROUGH what was waiting years ahead of me.

As my mom recited each verse, I visualized what she spoke.

> *"The Lord is my shepherd; I shall not want. He maketh me to lie down in green pastures; He leadeth me beside the still waters."*
>
> Psalm 23:1-2

Though I was very young at the time, preschool age, I imagined what it would be like to 'not want'. I pictured the beautiful and vibrant hue of the green pastures. I envisioned how I thought still waters would look, tranquil and serene.

> *"Yea, though I walk through the valley of the shadow of death, I will fear no evil; for thou art with me; thy rod and thy staff, they comfort me."*
>
> Psalm 23:4

I didn't like to think about the shadow of death's valley so instead I would imagine that there was most likely another way to the same destination. The author most likely just didn't know about it. Either way, it was comforting to know if I did have to go through that valley, I would fear no evil in the journey.

As a budding artist, and a young person unfamiliar with the King James translation, I relished in the thought that God was an artist as well. I liked that His *art* would be with me in case I needed something to occupy my time during my travels.

> *"Thou preparest a table before me in the presence of mine enemies; thou anointest my head with oil; my cup runneth over."*
>
> Psalm 23:5

I pictured the table and wondered why my enemies would even sit there if they didn't like me. I thought about the oil, how it might have felt, and whether it was similar to the grease my mom used on my hair. I wondered how big the cup was and why didn't God just stop pouring to keep it from running over. Who was going to clean up this mess God?

Even with all of that going on in my mind, as I listened to my mom's voice, my spirit would always settle down when she reached verse 6. My mom's name, before she changed it, was Shirley Mae. As a little girl, my mom's accent made it difficult to hear the difference between Shirley and surely. Goodness was good, mercy was nice, but I truly loved the idea that Shirley, goodness, and mercy would follow me all the days of my life, and that all of us, me, Shirley, goodness and mercy would dwell in the house of the Lord forever - together.

Throughout my childhood, those words carried me during the periods of change as my mom and I moved from one place to another. I depended on her for guidance, emotional support, protection, and provision; not expecting that she too was searching for someone on whom she could depend for the same things. From the age of 10, people told me that I had to look out for my mother, be supportive of her, and be the parent in the relationship. I took on my mother's abuse, her depression, and her self-pity; I internalized it and made it my own. The anger I felt towards her for her inability to be there for me I buried deep down so no one would see it. I felt no one would understand because everyone pitied her. I was told that God made me stronger than her and that He sent me to take care of her. Young and believing I was voiceless, I didn't know how to say, "I don't want to be strong. I don't want to be the parent. I don't want to take care of her. I want to be the child. I want my mother to love me." Instead, with my head bowed, my eyes lowered and my lips parted, I sat in capitulated silence.

My mom learned about Yoruba and the cultural practices through the people she met after we arrived in Washington, D.C. Popular among African Americans who wanted to connect in some way to the beliefs of their pre-New World ancestors, the practice was carried over to the Americas from its origins in Ghana and Nigeria, Africa. Rituals practiced include worshipping deities, performing animal sacrifices and body mutilation as part of initiation into the religion.

I'm sure what appealed to my mom was the instant acceptance and perceived love she felt from them. Her eagerness to be involved and to please them masked her vulnerability that stemmed from being unsure of herself in a new place, alone and without resources or family support. They became her family, welcomed her with open arms and gave her a new identity. They taught her to pray to the elements of the universe, worship orishas (minor gods in the Yoruba religion), and perform animal sacrifices to honor those beliefs. She changed her name to an African name and, in essence, tried to close the door to her past and mine as well.

When hurt is all you know, it is normal to want to look outward for a cause of the pain rather than to the inside for what needs to be changed or addressed. In her new religion, she believed the responsibility for what happened in her life had less to do with her, her actions or attitudes, and more, if not all, to do with the control and manipulation of the forces in the universe. Someone who feels broken will seek relief from outside sources because to believe the answers they seek are within implies that they themselves are either causing or perpetuating their own pain.

She relied wholeheartedly on the people she called her mentors in the religion and on the lady she called her godmother, who was the head of the temple we attended. We spent hours at the temple. On Sundays we'd go in at sunrise and not leave until long after sunset. Sunday service was more of an event or ceremony held weekly. At some point, a priestess would become possessed by an orisha and the next several hours would be spent catering to and receiving readings from the visiting spirit. The vessel or person the spirit chose to use to communicate through was then adorned in clothing and garb that represented that particular deity; white powder was sprinkled on his or her face which indicated the person was possessed.

Dinners at the temple were really the only time when I could understand why mother dedicated so much of her life to this new culture. When it was all over, the spirits had departed and those possessed had returned to their normal uneventful selves, we would all congregate around the table like a family. The higher officials, priestesses or kings remained in the main sanctuary and only certain women were permitted to handle the food. Culturally authentic foods were prepared and served: goat meat (from a sacrifice previously performed), chicken, fish, rice, plantains, and dishes like efo, fufu and ogbono soup. Traditional practices were also strictly adhered to such as serving the altars before any of us could eat.

She believed orishas were the rulers of the earth realm and the only way to succeed or have success in life was to put them first. When she prayed to the god of a particular element, she truly believed her prayers were being directed to God on her behalf. When her prayers did not manifest, she believed it was because the sacrifice had not been accepted. I suppose it was easier for her to pray to multiple idols and use their presumed displeasure as an excuse for her failures, never having to own up to the power and ability that God had already put inside her to be what He purposed for her to be. Instead she told me we needed to continue to pray and bring acceptable sacrifices to the gods. Even as a child, my spirit did not accept what she and her new circle of friends wanted me to believe.

This wasn't what God had intended for me. I refused to believe God wanted me to perform or sacrifice as my mom had decided to do. But how could I argue? First, I was a child who should be seen and not heard, and second, she genuinely seemed happy. The changes in her were noticeable and she seemed empowered by her new beliefs. I was happy for her; unfortunately, I didn't experience the same joy she did. Although her godmother was the head priestess and co-founder of the temple, the godmother's husband seemed only to tolerate his wife's practices. He visited the temple periodically and when he did, he was treated with the same respect as his wife.

My mom saw him as a father figure; she saw no issue in leaving me alone in his care at the temple while she ran errands. Perhaps she trusted he would treat me like a granddaughter or perhaps she entrusted me to watch out for myself. A day came when we both realized he didn't deserve her trust, nor did see me like a member of his family. His advance was subtle yet intentionally confident. The year before, my mom told me if a man ever touched my hand and tickled the center of it, I needed to get away from him, fast. When her godfather first took my hand, I thought nothing of it. But then I caught his stare and, with his eyes fixed on me, I immediately became uncomfortable. His finger slowly brushed the center of my palm. This was the tickle my mom warned me about. In that short span of time and space, I knew he didn't care that I was only 9 years old. What he wanted to do or have me do to him was nothing a man should want from a child. I pulled away from him and hid in the house until my mom returned.

As soon as I heard my mom's voice, I ran to tell her what happened. She then told her godmother. I am not sure what I expected to happen but what did happen, I truly didn't expect. The women of the temple, including my mom, decided nothing would be done or said to him. Instead the blame would be directed at me, the child. I was at fault for being around him. I, not he, not my mom, but I should have known better.

Child sexual abuse is more frequently found to occur in familiar environments, where the child is more trusting and afraid of standing up to someone they interact with on a regular basis. My mom's abuse was at the hands of a relative and mine began during playdates with children of people she asked to keep me. Around the same time of the incident at the temple, I was introduced to inappropriate sexual conduct but not from an adult. While playing 'house' with the children of my mom's friends, I was assigned the role of a parent which meant acting out with

NEVERTHELESS

another little girl the intimacies of a man and woman. They said I had to do it if I wanted to play with them. I had no one else my age to befriend. I was afraid saying "no" would mean ostracizing myself from the only friends I had. Despite feeling uncomfortable with the way we played or the things they told me to do, I didn't want to disappoint or cause them to be upset with me. I knew it was wrong but I felt all out of options.

Who could I confide in? I couldn't tell my mom that her friends' kids made me do things I didn't want to do. I told her about her godfather and nothing happened so why would this be any different? My mom was preoccupied with her own life and I didn't want to upset her with the things that I decided I could handle by holding inside. Instead, I began to separate myself from everyone else. I played in the hallway of the apartment building alone, which was easier than having to admit that I didn't like the games the other children played.

My mom would send me to the neighbor next door but since I had earned the title of a 'loner', it was normal to find me in the hall alone when I was supposed to be in the apartment next door to us. I knew my mom was home when I was sent to the neighbor's. I also knew why I was sent; so she could enjoy the company of her male friend. I didn't understand why I had to be sent to the next-door neighbor's home for her to have a visitor and part of the reason why I sat in the hallway right outside our apartment door was to catch a glimpse of him as he departed. I wanted to see the person whose attention was so important to my mom. Secretly, I hoped when he saw me, he'd want to stay to complete our family. I wanted him to love me like I thought he loved my mother and yet I had no idea if or how he loved her. I just knew she seemed happy when he was coming over and that I had to leave. I couldn't grasp why didn't he want to spend time with me too.

It was agony. Even as a young child, I wanted to close my eyes to life so the sad, loneliness would go away. It was like I was trapped inside a roller coaster car, alone to myself because I felt no one understood me or could rescue me from the isolation I carried. I wanted peace, happiness and joy but I didn't know how to find them. I wasn't even certain if they were available to me or if I was deserving of them. When would enough be enough?

NEVERTHELESS

Surprisingly, I thought this would be as hard as it would get. Yes, at 10 years old, I thought that was the worst of it. While other children my age were learning how to jump rope, ride a bike or participate in other social skills building activities, I was at the temple or alone. My job was to be out of the way but close enough to do as I was told. I wanted to be outside and away from it all but I obeyed and always remained just inside the fenced yard. Around this time is when people began saying I had an attitude problem. I was withdrawn, quiet and very reserved. I wasn't disrespectful or combative but because I chose not to accept what they wanted me to believe, they drew their own conclusions. This only caused me to withdraw more.

There was one place I could escape. My solace was school.

It was the only place where burning candles, beads, coconut shells and elaborate shrines decorated with bird feathers and the dried blood of sacrificed animals didn't dominate my life. I loved school and the normalcy I felt being around other children my age, as well as the satisfaction that soothed my soul when I received accolades from my teachers.

School was something I was good at and something I understood. I loved to learn but more than that, I loved how I felt when I had the right answer. I loved the attention and I hated to go home where the focus would no longer be on me or my accomplishments. The only challenge I faced adapting to school, teachers and other kids was that during my entire elementary level education I never attended the same school for more than two consecutive years. I was always starting over. I was always unsure, uncertain and insecure about fitting in with others. I was slowly drowning and looking up at the underside of the water's surface wondering if someone, anyone, would appear to grab my hand before the light faded into darkness.

I was slowly dying without love.

4

Some say hindsight is 20/20. Generally, the expression means looking back over a situation after it has been resolved and fully understanding where you went wrong. Once the err is identified and the actions which led to the mistake are evaluated, regret of decisions made soon follows. But for a believer, one who trusts God, steadfast and unmovable in their faith that all things work out for the good of those who trust Him, and are called according to His purpose, hindsight is not for reproof.

For one who puts all trust in God, looking back is simply to reveal that which was concealed, to praise for what God had already established, prepared, and planned for His glory and our THROUGH story.

But what about the unsaved?

God never said he only loves the saved, in fact, he loves the unsaved just the same because He is no respecter of persons. But it is what we do or fail to do in response to His love that determines how it manifests in our lives.

Almost every believer can quote John 3:16 *"God so loved the world that He gave His only Begotten Son, that whosoever believes in Him should not perish but have everlasting life."* But how many of us continue reading that same scripture until we reach verse 18, *"He who believes in Him is not condemned but he who does not believe is condemned already, because he had not believed in the name of the only begotten Son of God."*

We have been given a gift of God's love first, believer and non-believer, but what determines our relationship as a Child of God is our love of His Son.

"He who has My commandments and keeps them, it is he who loves Me. And he who

NEVERTHELESS

loves Me will be loved by My Father, and I will love him and manifest Myself to him."

John 14:21

He is a respecter of faith, and without faith, it is impossible to please Him. For both believer and nonbeliever, each can look back over their lives and see the hand of God, through mercy and grace. For me, although my mom had made her decision about who or what to worship, God continued to keep me and protect me knowing that one day I would come to Him on my own. He created for me a solace that I found in school, with teachers to love me when I needed it the most. But that wasn't all. God sent help in other ways too.

I am certain that regardless of how you were raised, whether as a Christian or another faith, you can identify people and places where God orchestrated a barrier of protection, a source of love and affection, and His Word was ministered to you to comfort you through the pain. This was for the relationship He knew you would one day have with Him and the glory of your testimony to help bring others out of a similar darkness.

When I was 8 or 9 years old, it was suggested to my mom that she enroll me in the Big Brother Big Sister (BBBS) program. Originated in New York in 1904, the BBBS works to establish mentoring relationships between children of single parent homes and adult role models. The goal is the minimize the likelihood that a child who is at risk will succumb to the hardships of life. The impact of my time in the program was something I was able to pull from and remember for the rest of my life, and it helped to shape me into the woman I am today.

To describe Jill and her husband Jeff, the first white people I was allowed to spend time with, in one word, I would have to say "Woodstock". With my mom consumed by her new African traditions and practices, I was surprised she agreed to let me have a white woman as a big sister. I think it helped that they were modest and looked as if they spoke only of peace and love. But the biggest shocker over her agreeing to let Jill be my 'Big' was that I was permitted to engage in Christian celebrations with them.

NEVERTHELESS

This was ALL God. He sent a loving couple, to cross racial barriers, to show me that love can come from anyone, and not to be biased by race or predisposed to the pains of the opinions of my mom and her beliefs. Jill and Jeff took me to church with them, taught me how to ride a bike they purchased for me from a secondhand store, took me to visit their family and truly loved me. They lived in a studio basement apartment and wore clothes that were shabby but they had an abundance of love they were willing to share with me. They taught me love by showing me love. And everything we did, we did together. When she asked if I wanted pizza, I knew it meant we were going to make everything from scratch, including the dough and sauce, and that we would go to the market for fresh veggies. Once I made the mistake of saying I wanted to make brownies with walnuts. When she pulled out the sledge hammer I would need to crack the shells of the nuts, I quickly said, "Oh, plain will do."

I will never forget sneaking into the kitchen to get a taste of the chocolate melting in the pot on the stove. I grabbed the largest spoon I could find, filled it with the warm watery chocolate, and put the entire scoop of sauce in my mouth. That day, I learned a valuable lesson: chocolate can be sugarless.

For Christmas that year, I wanted a doll and I felt comfortable enough to ask Jill for it. It would be my only gift since there was no tree or gift exchange going to happen at my house.

My mom allowed me to go with Jill to her parents' home in Ohio. It was wonderful. We sang Christmas songs in the car, ate granola, and played road trip games the entire way. Her parents were just as beautiful and I knew from where Jill had gotten her lovingkindness. But all I could think about was the doll I wanted and asked her for. When it came time to open presents, she handed me a box that couldn't possibly hold a doll, at least not the doll I had asked for. I held my breath as I opened it. But when I saw what was in the box, I couldn't hide my disappointment. For the first time in years, since leaving Charlotte, I had permitted myself to be hopeful and happily expectant only to be regretfully sadden.

Inside the box wasn't a doll at all. Well, sort of. It was filled with all the things that had the potential to be a doll. She gifted me a doll sewing pattern for us to make a doll from scratch. I was quiet for the entire ride home.

I could tell my disappointment had hurt her feelings but I couldn't help it. I wanted what I wanted. I was a child, immature in my ways and lacking the full understanding of what she was teaching me. She had given me all the pieces to have what I wanted but I couldn't see the beauty in that gift. I didn't want to work for it. I wanted it like everyone had theirs, from the store, and with a certain look. I was a child but how many of us can say, we are still like this as adults? Unyielding in our desires. Not putting the love of God first in our wants or second, in our responses.

God has given us all the pieces to have what we want. In His love, He has given us patience, kindness, strength, friendship, trust, forgiveness and victory. But sometimes we fail to operate in the beauty of this gift. We want what we want, like children, to be like others and if we don't get it then we open the door to the enemy's deceptive notions that we think we aren't truly loved. When we fall, we feel worthless as if we don't possess the power to forgive ourselves and get back up. We fall prey to unforgiveness and guilt, putting on ourselves a condemnation that Christ has redeemed us from on the Cross.

There's beauty in the lesson and it comes with a promise, but we have to be willing to go through the process of sowing love always. Sometimes the process may not even seem like it is for us, but that's not the point. The lesson for ourselves and others is HOW we go through it. Are we bitter, resentful, angry or are we patient, long-suffering, joyful and at peace knowing that *"all things work together for the good to those who love God, to those who are the called according to His purpose"* as it is written in Romans 8:28? The amazing ability and power of God's love is that it blesses us as we are being a blessing to others. By giving, we receive.

I could have remained bitter and pouted until I got what I wanted but I didn't. I loved her and she loved me. She didn't deserve the attitude I was giving her and it wasn't making me feel any better about myself. I had to fix it. Not for me but I would go through the doll-making process because she wanted us to. It took some time to complete the doll. I had to pick out fabric, the right shade I wanted for the skin, yarn for the hair, stuffing, clothes, etc. Shockingly, I actually began to enjoy myself. Who knew??!!!

By the end, I was pleased and grateful that we worked on my doll together. My doll was an original, no other would ever exist like my doll. She was special. She was beautiful because I created her to look like me. This doll meant more to me after everything it took to make it than any other doll ever would or could. If this doll could mean this much to me, how special do you think we are to God? We are beautiful; we are fearfully and wonderfully made and in His image.

I still have my doll today.

Jill and her husband accepted a mission ministry assignment that relocated them to Botswana, Africa. It hurt to see her leave but I had a piece of her to hold on to. I didn't realize how many times I would turn to my doll for comfort, how many times I would hold it as I cried or how many times I would talk to it as if I were talking to Jill. Turned out that I needed that doll more than I realized. The gift that Jill gave me wasn't about the activities we did together or the places we visited. God used Jill to teach me about relationships. Through my experience and time with Jill as my Big and with me as her Little, I learned a lot about what type of person I wanted to be. Jill didn't have flashy material things but she was able and willing to love me, and she *wanted* to spend time with me. Her love felt genuine. She believed what she was doing would make a difference in my life, and it did.

After Jill left the program to move to Botswana, the BBBS program assigned me another volunteer big sister. I hoped for another Jill. I got Holly. I tried to have the same relationship with her as I had with Jill. Except she was nothing like Jill. Like Jill, Holly was white, married and childless. That's where the similarities ended.

Holly and her husband lived in an upper-class neighborhood of Northwest Washington, D.C. She drove a 2-door Porsche Carrera and owned a pure-bred Sharpei which I thought was the funniest looking dog I'd ever seen. Her home was a 3-story townhouse with high ceilings and furniture that I wasn't allowed to sit on. When she came to my house to pick me up, it was obvious that she wasn't comfortable. She drew a tremendous amount of attention stepping out of her expensive car, draped in a full-length fur coat and sneakers. It was embarrassing. I longed for Jill and her old mint green sedan.

I want to believe that Holly had the best intentions. To take on the role of big sister and commit at least a year of your life to mentoring a young person is a great responsibility. It requires time, effort, financial resources, and can be emotionally draining. But there's one requirement that she couldn't fake: a true desire for a loving relationship with me.

Our relationships in the natural should resemble and imitate our relationship with our Heavenly Father. He created us to be in relationship with one another because He is the creator of relationship. But it requires pure love for godly kind of relationship. Not in physical intimacy but in heart. God is the master relationship-maker and sustainer, and it is only natural that our relationships be modeled after

His example. Regardless of marital status, whether or not you have children, and unless you are a hermit who has never met another living soul, we are all in relationship with another, and those relationships have requirements. They represent something in our lives that is either gained or lost and has returns that are either invested into our spirit or reinvested into the spirit of the relationship. Whether it is a brief encounter with someone you've only met once in your life, a glance around the room until your eyes meet up with another person for only a second before turning away, or an 80-year marriage that has produced ten kids, 30 grandkids and 100 great-grands, those are all relationships in one form or another.

It is important to remove any inconvenience from the picture and seek direction from Holy Spirit because that exchange may be about a need greater than just a simple hello. A person could very well be a friendly person who receives joy from interacting with others or someone facing a life or death decision due to thoughts of suicide or depression, with one negative response or attitude from you adversely changing their life in that split-second encounter. This is where we must remember that our

NEVERTHELESS

relationships represent something greater than ourselves.

Again, just as in life long relationships, brief encounters are an opportunity to show who we represent, what that encounter represents, and how important the person we are interacting with is to us because they are important to the Kingdom of God. Once we accept Christ as Lord, we are no longer representatives of ourselves. To take on the cover of God, the protection of God, the peace of God, we must also understand that we take on the responsibility of doing and being the representation of Christ in the earth.

The brave persons who serve in the military have no problem representing this country and dedicating their lives. Bikers have no problem wearing the colors of their motorcycle ministries or clubs, knowing that there are certain behaviors and expectations that those colors demand. But when it comes to carrying our own crosses for Christ, Christians have so many issues with submitting to His Word unconditionally and unequivocally. There's hesitation in accepting the required behavior changes and living up to the expectations of unfailing love. There seems to always be exceptions to just how the picture looks of our representation of the greater One living on the inside of us. Yet, it all still comes down to relationships and what we are willing to do for them.

How important are your relationships to you? How important are your friendships? What about your marriage, your connection to your children, nieces, nephews, and God-children? How important is your connection to your parents? But above all those, how important is your relationship with God? He has given us the greater connector, His Son Jesus. God has given us the ultimate covenant maker and there's no other relationship that can ever compare. It is the example made flesh in the earth for us to follow, *"love one another; as I have loved you, that you also love one another."* (*John 13:34*)

Jill understood this commandment and it was as if she sowed the seed for this kind of love in my heart. This seed would eventually make room for the Word of God to deliver me; eventually opening the door to the love of Jesus to come into my life.

NEVERTHELESS

"The He spoke many things to them in parables, saying: "Behold, a sower went out to sow. And as he sowed, some seed fell by the wayside; and the birds came and devoured them.

Some fell on stony places, where they did not have much earth; and they immediately sprang up because they had no depth of earth. But when the sun was up they were scorched, and because they had no root they withered away.

And some fell among thorns, and the thorns sprang up and choked them. But others fell on good ground and yielded a crop: some a hundredfold, some sixty, some thirty."

Matthew 13:3-8

My match with Holly didn't last and my mom decided not to try for a third time.

Soon after, I finished 6th grade and instead of fond memories of celebrating my graduation from elementary school, my mom and I found ourselves homeless. We were evicted and all our belongings were placed on the street for the world to see.

Evictions are not just embarrassing because the entire neighborhood sees you as poor, but also because the people hired to evict you only care about the task at hand. They aren't paid to be gentle or kind; they're paid to get us out and to do it as quickly as possible.

Coming home to find all our belongings on the street was extremely unnerving for me as a child. How could I ever feel safe and settled when at any time a group of men could come into our home and throw everything we had out on the street? What I didn't realize then was that evictions didn't come by surprise. Instead, it is a process that a landlord must follow and notices are given in advance of the dreadful day. Once I learned an eviction could be planned for, I never understood why or how we were unprepared, why didn't we move before the eviction was scheduled or better yet, make arrangements to pay. Either way, preparation wasn't something my mom was afforded and our belongings were subjected to gawkers and looters determined to make an already dire situation worse. She was unaware that the money she paid to her friend, whom she shared the lease, wasn't being paid to the homeowner. Coming home to all our

NEVERTHELESS

possessions set out on the street was just as much a disbelief to her as it was to me.

Lacking anywhere else to go, my mom sent me to Miami to live with her girlfriend who had three girls of her own. It was only supposed to be for the summer, to give her time to get back on her feet. She said, "Be a good girl. I will see you in a few weeks." But a few weeks turned into a few months. Her friend was forced to enroll me in my first year of middle school with no preparation, financial assistance or enrollment paperwork. With school clothes purchased at the local thrift store, I was ready for 7th grade.

When my mom returned to pick me up that following January. I didn't care why she left me or how long she had been away, I was happy she had returned. I dreamed every night that her love would force her to come back for me. When she did, her loved was confirmed in me like the hold of an addiction that the next high would be the best one yet. Our life in Charlotte was still a fresh memory that I held onto one day becoming reality again. I pictured our time apart was as hard for her as it was for me and that while I was away, she had acquired a place for just us. I wanted it to be just us again. I wanted our family back. I wanted our relationship back and the love we shared, I wanted it back more than anything else. The love from Jill, where I felt as if she truly enjoyed being with me, reminded me of my life with my mom back in Charlotte. That is why it was so dear to me. It was my mom who had planted the seed of love and it was Jill who nurtured it.

When our bus pulled into Union Station in D.C., I couldn't be happier to be home. Everything was familiar and I was optimistic for what my mom had accomplished while I was in Miami. I imagined our new place, reserved just for the two of us where we could once again begin our lives together, to conquer the world protecting and loving one another more than anyone else could ever do. Instead, we arrived at the apartment of yet another friend. In the 600 s.f. space already lived three people and a dog. Although not properly insulated to legally qualify as a bedroom, the enclosed back porch was where I would sleep. The makeshift bed consisted of a mattress atop a twin-size board supported by milk crates. The dresser was lodged between the mattress and the wall with just enough room to barely access the drawers and the door to the room was directly across from the backdoor. Once I was settled in, my mom left.

Again, I was left to the care of someone else, this time so she could take a job as a live-in nanny to a family in Chicago. "Be a big girl and make mommy proud," she said. I had heard those words so many times and I knew what they really meant, "don't complain...don't make trouble". Looking back, I can see now that this point in my life was the crossroad where an intervention was needed most. I began to hate how I felt about love. I hated that I still loved and longed for love from my mom. I even hated longing for my father, a man whom I'd never met but believed should have been in my life. I hated that Jill left me and that Holly couldn't love me. I didn't understand why those who mattered to me chose not to remain in my life.

What did I have to do? What wasn't I doing right? Why was I unworthy? Where was this god that my mom worshiped, prayed, and made animal sacrifices to for covering? Had God forgotten about me? Had my mom finally figured out how to live her life without her only child? I needed my mom. I needed to know I was loved.

5

M iddle school is such a pivotal and demonstrative period in a child's life. Colliding the pubescent dysfunction of preteen years with greater responsibility and expectation of maturity is simply a recipe for disaster on so many levels. Children who have not fully accepted their transition from the senior level of elementary school to the position of middle school "freshmeat" are now subjected to the 8th graders who have waited an entire year for this moment. Middle school juniors were finally able to subject the same pains that were inflicted upon them the year prior upon someone new, and the ninth graders who have propelled themselves to a godlike level of superiority, acted as if everyone wanted to be them and never would.

While my mom lived in Chicago working as a nanny to another woman's child, I attempted to do as I was told, "Be a good girl." I wanted to make her happy but the longing for my own personal love and affection grew stronger and deeper. I tried to do exactly what she asked of me but I was beginning to believe that I didn't matter to her. If what I wanted didn't matter to her, then why should what she wanted matter to me? Eventually, I began to feel as if I deserved an explanation. But I couldn't bring myself to ask for one. I had to stay in a child's place. I had to be a good girl. I had to make my mom proud.

Everything changed when I asked why couldn't I come to stay with her while she cared for someone else's child. She told me it was the decision of her employer. I didn't understand why she didn't quit on the spot. It was difficult to accept that someone perceived me as a distraction, but it was more upsetting that my mom accepted it.

After that, I no longer cared if my mom came back. I didn't want to be her good girl and I didn't

NEVERTHELESS

care if I made her proud. She had a new family. I would find someone else to care about me. I was now 13 years old and decided it was the perfect time to take advantage of the attention I often received.

As a child, whenever I would complain about how things were, my mom would reply that I chose her. She believed children, as spirits, choose who they want to come into the world through. At the risk of a backhanded slap to the mouth, I replied, "What were my other choices?" With my body developing into the fullness of a woman, and the fact that all the 'cool' kids at my school were sexually active, I decided the only way to gain someone's love was to give up that which can only be given once. I thought it would prove I was worth loving and would validate my existence. In the 8th grade, I gave away my virginity; I did so with the hope of receiving the same exchange of love that I envisioned my mom received while I sat on those hallway stairs.

There was nothing special about the man I allowed to share my first encounter. He pulled up alongside me driving a green convertible Peugeot, asked for my name and my age. I told him my name and that I was sixteen. He said he was eighteen. We both lied. I didn't have a phone number to give him because I wasn't allowed to receive calls from boys, especially ones who drove a car and were eighteen. Communication was tricky. This was before cellphones were common place and long before social media. He had a pager and told me to page him later that day. Before I could page him, however, I had to make sure to be on another call when he called back. With call waiting, it was the only way to avoid the phone ringing and someone else answering the phone.

The first night we spoke, he asked if I could come back outside and if we could go to the movies later. It was already after my bedtime but I said yes.

Two hours later, there I was, in his car and on my way to a late-night movie with a guy I had just met. It was exciting; the wind blowing through my hair and the stars bright in the night sky above. The slow jams played on his radio and all sorts of emotions ran through my body, my skin tingled and I felt alive. I don't recall the movie we saw that evening but I remember he turned to me and said he wanted me to be his. It was the strangest feeling to be told someone wanted me. Although we had just met, I wanted to believe him. I was so lost in the entire experience that I believed it had to be love. Finally, I thought, someone wanted me. Our next date was our encounter. I remember the pain. I remember wondering where were the sparks and fireworks. I remember being unimpressed. Even worse, I remember feeling empty. Soon after, the relationship dissolved and I learned it only added to the void I felt before I gave myself to him.

Other relationships came and went, and with each relationship and sexual encounter, my self-worth went with it. I started being truant from school, hanging with girls who got a lot of attention from guys and I met the expectations of what was required of me to be with them. I was living a reckless life. I was on a path of destruction and no one was watching me close enough to see it.

For a young girl, promiscuity is a cry for help. In the community where I grew up, sexual indiscriminate behavior among teens was common and therefore went unaddressed. Teenage girls in my neighborhood viewed being sexually active as a way of asserting themselves as adults, and as a way of taking control of their lives when everything else seemed out of control. Most of the families consisted of children raised by single parent mothers or grandparent guardians receiving government assistance. Everything was a struggle and everyone was on some sort of "come up" or hustle. Young boys sold drugs and young girls gave an exchange of sex for their material and emotional needs. As young boys helped to support their mothers by selling drugs, young girls helped by having babies. As converse as adding a dependent to a home with extreme lack may seem, emancipation by pregnancy meant that teenagers would qualify for government assistance in a home already receiving assistance. For example, a home initially receiving funds for one family became a home receiving funds for two families under the same roof. Income to the home increased as well as food stamps, which were also sold for 50 cents on the dollar. Like I said, there was always a hustle.

At the end of the school day, drug dealers would line their cars up along T Street in front of Langley Junior High and McKinley Technical Senior High to pick up their teenage girlfriends. Any girl who wasn't sexually active held her virginity close as if it was a shameful secret. While it was strange when a 7th grade classmate became pregnant and kept her baby, it was less surprising that almost every girl I knew had either aborted a baby or contracted a sexually transmitted disease before the age of 16. It was a downward spiral that I struggled to find a way of escape. There were times when I felt like my soul had left my body, was hovering above me watching what I was allowing to happen to me, only to return to my body once the act was completed.

Each time I hoped it would be different than the last time. I thought I would rise and be whole. Instead of completing me, though, each time I laid there, I ended up feeling diminished in esteem and in hope. I was an addict who was addicted to the hope of better, the hope of love and acceptance of self but too weak to see that same the addiction that kept me bound would never be the catalyst to propel me upward. From the first encounter, I had grown dependent upon the intimacy and the physical connection that allowed me temporary relief from my depression and feelings of rejection. The lustful desire I received from men, young and old, gave me a false sense of empowerment. This wasn't love nor was it healthy but I thought it was the best I could create for myself.

My mom eventually learned of my sexual activity and after complaints of my behavior from the people I lived with, she moved back to D.C. She demanded to meet the boy I gave my virginity to, as if speaking to him would portray her as the protector I needed her to be prior to the event. I introduced her to him and he introduced her to his mom. They discussed everything without me present. She informed them of my age and learned that he was a 21 year old man who was now facing charges of statutory rape of a minor but she never pressed charges. Upset and disappointed, she went days without speaking to me. The person I believed had unconditional love for me was disappointed in me. I felt like nothing. There was only one thing left for me to do. Be nothing and exist no longer.

I decided if she didn't love me anymore, because of what I had done, then what was the point of living to see another day? During a visit at the home of one of my mom's friends, I excused myself to the bathroom, opened the medicine cabinet and grabbed the only bottle I saw. I filled a glass with water and swallowed as many pills as I could. Realizing how long I had been in the bathroom, the friend came to check on me and found the empty bottle of pills in my hand. She yelled for my mother and began forcing her finger down my throat which caused me to regurgitate most of what I had swallowed. They discussed calling 911 but decided against it because a report to the authorities would draw unwanted attention from social services and potentially lead to child protective authorities investigating our family. They nursed me back to health and that night I paid a pretty painful price for the decision I had made. Because I survived, I considered myself a failure and yet the irony was I hoped my mom would finally see how much I needed her. For a brief while after the decision to take my own life, I thought things had changed because my mom was more attentive to me.

It was short lived.

While my mom had her deities and orishas, I was left with my memories. I settled on the notion that everyone leaves eventually. No one stays. Love was painful and sex was the only token I had to offer in exchange for a counterfeit form of affection. Love and affection, the desire of it was my drug. I sought it but didn't understand it well enough to know what it was or how it looked. A greater void was created each time I opened myself up to receive love because each person I trusted to honor me lovingly only sought out to use me. This was my valley of the shadow of death, and I feared evil tremendously. I was lost and afraid. I was in a valley of deception and destruction and yet the words of the 23rd Psalm would often come to mind. I didn't understand the power of God's Word planted on the inside of me. The confidence that comes from knowing God is with us, God has never left us, God loves us and even in our darkest days, is a power that the enemy does not want us to realize. Satan wants us to fear although God did not give us a spirit of fear.

In fact, God tells us many times in the Scripture to 'fear not' and yet out of ignorance of His Word and lacking a relationship with Him, I was afraid. I did live in fear and pursued my own sense of security and safety. God does not expect or require us to attempt to develop or even manage our own security and safety. In the natural, I'm not saying it is unnecessary

NEVERTHELESS

have home insurance or security service, but rather we shouldn't put more faith in external sources of security than we do in our faith in God for all things supernatural. While God tells us in James 4:7, we are to submit to Him, resist the devil and then the devil will flee. It is His Word and our submission to it that allows us the strength and the confidence to know that our resistance is backed by God, and because the enemy is no match for God's Word when activated by our faith, he must flee. Unfortunately, people don't read the first part of the verse and assume just claiming to resist the enemy will be enough. When fear, doubt, and pain continue to present in our lives, we begin to waver and focus on trying to correct our situations by our own hands.

I was still in need of love. I was still in need of my mom. But now I was attempting to replace or substitute the love I needed and longed for from her with sexual encounters. Being a good girl for my mom while she was away didn't work. My attempt to take my life didn't work. What I never expected to happen, which was feeling even more empty and alone, was now a dreadful reality for my life. At 13, I was no longer a virgin and the man I had given my virginity was out of my life just as quickly as he had come into it. At 13 I saw myself not even worthy of my mom's love and protection. Without the strength of God that comes from His Word, I wasn't equipped to resist the enemy. Without understanding of the requirement to submit to God, I was left thinking I could, on my own, protect myself.

Comparing how empty, used, and unwanted I felt during that period of my life, I am reminded of a rowboat I saw during a tube ride down the Antietam Creek in Sharpsburg, Maryland. The rowboat, which was tied to a tree root that extended out from the side of the river, had seen better days. As I floated down the creek, I watched it hit against the rocks with a beat that matched the rhythmic flow of the waves. Hoping the owner was nearby, I imagined the little vessel as a living person with feelings and a personality. I thought about how it would feel as a person, left abandoned by the riverside and a sense of loneliness overtook me. I thought about how it might have looked when it was brand new not yet introduced to the cold temperatures of the river, the hardness of the rocks that sometimes could not be avoided or how excited the owner might have been the first time the boat was placed in the water. I thought about how it might have shined in the sunlight as rays peeked through the treetops or how others who sailed by in lessor valued versions would envy what this little rowboat had.

I had no idea of its age, owner or the number of times it had traveled up and down that particular river or others. What I knew was what I saw, a boat left vulnerable and subjected to anything or anyone who happened by. Made for a purpose, it now sat by the riverbend waiting to be used again. I closed my eyes and rested my head back against the side of the plastic tube trying to forget about that little raggedy rowboat but instead of forgetting it, I began counting all the ways in which the rowboat and me had in common. I imagined there must have been a time when someone was excited to have me, to know me and to be with me. From the love of a new parent to the love of a boyfriend in a new relationship, I remembered what it felt like to be held in a loving embraced, even if temporarily. Then I painfully remembered what it felt like to be abandoned, no longer wanted or desired; I felt the loneliness of the rowboat swell up inside me.

As tears began to collect in the corners of my closed eye lids, I exchanged the image of the boat tied to the riverside with the image of me, I was now bound to the rocks waiting to be used and then discarded. I thought about the partners who had come and gone and the gift I gave of my body in the hope of gaining love and commitment in return. I thought about how worn and empty I felt; how much I wanted to disappear into an air or nothingness, never to be seen or heard from again. I remembered wanting to be free from the pain but not knowing how, where or who to turn. Everyone I turned to hoping for help only ended up wanted to use me for their pleasure or gain. I wondered if the rowboat ever came to life and experienced feelings, would it long to be free like I did as a child? If it ever came untethered from the tree root that held it secure against the current of the river, what would come of it? Without guidance, without care, without someone who knows how to navigate the conditions before us, without someone who has our best interests and purpose in heart, an unmanned journey would undoubtedly end in destruction.

So where do we turn?

NEVERTHELESS

The Word of God is our navigation and guide, the protection and provision for our lives and purpose. Without it, without knowledge of it we perish. We all have purpose, we all have been secured by a price that is greater than all things. God can take us where we are and equip us to do great and mighty in His Kingdom. We just have to agree and be open to seeing ourselves as the treasures we are and worthy of being loved.

Me in junior high.

6

Death. "Without love, the soul dies." Seems like a catchy phrase or song verse, right? Sure, it's catchy but also true.

In *KevinMD's* March 17, 2014 blog post, Dr. Pamela Wible shares why she believes "people die without love". While lack of love can be connected to a natural demise, it can also cause a supernatural death as well. Knowing God is love and viewing death as representation of separation, we can see that without revelation and understanding of His love, we are denying our souls from ever being reunited in the victory that Christ has redeemed for us. I call this a 'soul-ish' death, where we are still living in the natural but are existing in a realm of nothingness that can only be resurrected by faith in the Word of God and revelation of the love of Christ.

> *"... and though I have all faith, so that I could remove mountains, but have not love, I am nothing."*
>
> 1 Corinthians 13:2

Looking back over my life, I tried to pinpoint the moment when I died a soul-ish death and I determined it happened when I was 14 years old. My mom and I had been through our share of trials and yet I still had hope in her to love and support me. I felt up to that point, I had been able to endure all that had happened to me in my life, from abuse from others to depression and abandonment, but was certain that if anything occurred that I was unable to handle, my trust and hope was in her to protect me. I still desired her to be the rock I needed and had not fully accepted her weaknesses.

By 1989, my mom had secured a place for us to live together. I didn't have many friends because I was still relatively new to this area of D.C., having only moved to Third and T Streets a year earlier. I knew one girl who lived around the corner from me only because she was in my 8th grade homeroom class. We weren't close and because she was as equally awkward as I was and just as much a magnet for bullying, I purposely didn't spend that much time seeking out her company. I was an only child and was used to doing things by myself. Like walking to the corner store.

My outfit was a perfect reflection of the weather and the beauty of the cloudless day. I wore a peach colored knee length skirt set and sandals. My hair, braided in human hair individuals, was pulled back into a ponytail to showcase the new $5 earrings I had gotten earlier that week from the beauty supply store. The clerk said they would last for at least a whole week before they began to turn green. I looked forward to one day being able to buy those hypoallergenic ones because they lasted longer, according to the Vietnamese clerk behind the counter.

With soda and chips in hand, I started my trip in reverse and headed back to the apartment where my mom and I lived. She was home and that's probably why I was so determined to go to the store. My steps were slow and deliberately hesitant because

I didn't want to go back in the house so soon. My mom and I weren't getting along and being in the same 1-bedroom apartment with her was often times unbearable. All I kept thinking to myself was "oh well, this trip was for nothing. She's not going to let me out again until tomorrow." And then I heard the question I think every girl will have heard over 1 trillion times in her lifetime, "Excuse me, can I talk to you for a minute?" There it was, a *something*, and an *anything* to keep me from having to go back in the house right away. I turned and said, "Sure."

His name was Johnny and he said he had seen me in the neighborhood. We walked in the direction of my home and once we got to my apartment building he asked for my phone number so he could call me sometime. I said yes but I knew if I went in the house, my mom would not allow to go back out and surely not to give my number to a boy. He motioned to the end of the block and said he could go to his house and get paper and a pen for me to write my number. I agreed to go with him. First mistake.

I knew the building well enough only because it was the largest multifamily building in the neighborhood. Most buildings including the one I lived in were 2-story garden style units but his building was at least six floors. There were always people standing out front and when he told me to follow him so I wouldn't be out front alone, I thought how kind it was that he cared enough to want to protect me from that scene. I agreed to walk inside the building, followed him one level down to the basement floor where his apartment was located. Second mistake.

I stopped at the door to his unit so he could go inside. With my hand holding the door to the apartment open, I got the first glimpses inside the small apartment. The door opened into the kitchen that had a café size table near the door. From the doorway I could see two small rooms, one in which he went to get paper. He returned to the kitchen, put the paper on the table and turned to hand me the pen. Without realizing it meant stepping inside, in a split second I made mistake number three.

Now inside the apartment, I grabbed the pen, releasing the door and immediately it closed with a loud slam behind me. The sound of the door startled me but I tried to hide the fear that crept up inside. He handed me the pen and I wrote down my number and address. I thought it was strange for him to ask for my address, but I wrote it down as requested. When I finished, I handed him the pen and turned to follow him as he walked past me to the door. But instead of reaching for the doorknob like I expected, he reached for the keyed deadbolt and with one turn of the key, I was trapped inside. He removed the key from the lock and placed it in his pocket.

In an instant my world changed. He didn't like me. He wanted to hurt me. He only wanted to use me. He was a liar. He was evil.

"What are you doing?"

"Look, I just want a hug. Just give me a hug and I'll let you go."

"Please don't do this."

"Just hug me then".

"You promise to open the door if I hug you."

"Yeah."

NEVERTHELESS

I hugged him but he didn't let me go. "You promised, please let me go." I pleaded.

"Now I want a kiss."

"Please don't do this to me. Why are you doing this? I thought you liked me." I managed to say between sobs.

He said, "I do like you, that's why I want you to kiss me."

"But I don't want to." I said as I slowly back away from him but the room was so small and in two steps I had reached the wall. The tears felt warm as they fell down my cheeks but I tried to wipe them away quickly so not to show the fear that I felt engulfing me. He saw my tears and, for a brief moment, I thought my luck had changed because he then left the room. Perhaps he had an ounce of compassion after all, perhaps he was going to let me go. But as quickly as the glimmer of hope came upon me, it dissipated once I saw what he was holding in his hand when he returned. Down by his side was a wooden bat. I dropped down to the floor and crouched in a seated position holding my knees to my chest. Too afraid to be hysterical but not strong enough to keep from crying, I begged and pleaded with him to let me go. But he just smiled at me and it made my stomach turn.

"Look, it's up to you. Either you can kiss me or you can sit there until you fall asleep and then I am going to beat you with this bat. So just kiss me so I can let you go."

"You promise? If I just kiss you, you'll let me leave?"

"Yea, I promise." He lied.

I got up off the floor and walked up to him, shuddering at the thought of putting my lips to his. I extended my face to his face, my lips to his lips, and just as the flesh of my lips touched his, he wedged his tongue into my mouth, forcing my lips apart with the thrust. I cringed and drew away from him, disgusted but hopeful the ordeal was over.

"Okay," I said as I withdrew from him, "now please let me go."

"I can't."

NEVERTHELESS

"Why not!" At that moment, I knew if I wanted to go home and pretend none of this ever happened, that I would have to give him what he wanted. I wasn't stupid and I wasn't a virgin. Though I was only 14 years old, I had been given that same lustful and perverted stare by both old and young men, trusted father figures and strangers, so I knew exactly what he wanted from me.

With the bat in one hand, he said, "Look at what you done to me." He pointed down to his crotch. "You got me hard and now I can't let you leave me this way." Then he said, "It's not like you haven't done it before. I know some of the dudes you screwed so you can just do it to me too. It is up to you. You can give me some and just go home."

It was as if he had done this before.

He continued, "Besides, no one knows you're here anyway so no one will come looking for you."

He was right. I should have obeyed my mom. I should have gone home. I thought about my mom and how mad she was going to be at me for being out so late when I was supposedly only going to the store.

The longer I held out, the more trouble I was going to be in. Thinking only of my mom, about how much trouble staying out was going to cause and feeling more afraid of her than of him, I looked at him and said, "Okay."

He led me to one of the small rooms off from the kitchen where I would give him what he wanted so he would let me go. Like he said, I was no stranger to 'IT'. But this time 'IT' was worse. I was accustomed to the emotional void that came with 'IT', but I struggled to comprehend threatening someone's life just to have 'IT'.

I removed my skirt, then my top, and then my cartoon alligator undershirt and matching shorts. I laid on the mattress, closed my eyes and waited for him to enter me. I wanted it to be over. Eventually, I began to stare up at the ceiling as a way of separating myself from what was happening. I laid there listening to the sounds of his heavy breathing in my ear as the movement from the body on top of me repeated for a brief period of time, before ending unceremoniously. Though it seemed like an eternity, in reality it was less than five minutes for him to finish. Immediately the guilt and shame began to sink in.

I picked my clothes up off the floor, looked at my alligator underwear and wondered if his semen was going to come out of me into my underwear and ruin them. I would have to throw them away. I hated him even more because I loved that set. Then I began to worry over what was I going to tell my mother about me being out so late. I couldn't tell her what had just happened because it was my fault. I went to his apartment when I should have gone home, I went inside the door instead of walking away and I gave myself to him instead of fighting back. I constantly berated myself with, *"If only I had allowed him to hit me, beat me, kill me then at least I wouldn't have to live with the shame of giving in to his abuse"*. It was difficult for me to accept my decision to give in to him. The scene did not play out as I had watched on the big screen countless times before, by actors portraying the horrific moments of a violent rape. I wondered if an offense had even transpired.

As I dressed, he gave me his demands. He said I had to come back every day and do it again. Instead of going to school, I would have to come to his apartment and have sex with him. If I didn't, he would come up to my school and tell everyone that I was a whore. He said my life would be ruined and that he would make sure of it. But I could avoid all of that if I agreed to come back each day. Then he held up the piece of paper that I had written my phone number and address on and said, "Remember, I know where to find you."

Considering what I had already done and given him for my freedom, agreeing verbally to the rest of his demands was easy to do. I knew I wouldn't come back. I would die before I came back. Feeling triumphant, he retrieved the key, inserted it into the cylinder and unlocked the door. The sound of the mechanism unlocking was as loud to me as the sound of the door slamming shut earlier. Except this time, the sound would be one of liberation rather than confinement.

The one-block walk was horrible. It had gotten dark fast and seemed as if I had been gone all day. I walked quickly to get as much distance between me and what had just happened but with each step, I

NEVERTHELESS

dreaded what I was going to say to my mom. What would I tell her? The pain between my legs from the unwanted intercourse paled in comparison to what I feared I would receive as punishment for being out late, without permission.

Scrambled thoughts raced through my mind as I walked home. *I should lie. I can't tell anyone. She won't believe me anyway. It was my fault. She's going to be so mad. I can't tell her. But I NEED to tell her. I have to tell her. Please mom, please don't be mad at me.*

As soon as I turned the knob, my mom was at the door fuming in disbelief. She yelled, "Where have you been?!"

"Mommy," I said as I fell onto her body, "he raped me."

The moments that followed my declaration were surreal. I struggled with believing it was rape because I had said *yes*. Did I want to? No. Did I believe I was trapped? Yes. Did I believe I was in danger? YES. Doubt had set in and I didn't know how to take those thoughts captive. I was trying to hold on to the little power I had left, the power that came from telling my mom the truth. I felt powerless during the assault but I was getting my power back now by choosing not to allow him to further the abuse me or control me after the assault.

My mom called the police. They arrived and took a report. I was taken by ambulance to the emergency room of Children's Hospital and a rape examination was conducted. In the emergency room, pictures were taken of my face, hands and arms, and my clothes were bagged and kept as evidence. Hair was pulled from my scalp as well as my genital area, my finger nails were clipped and kept as well. I was given a pelvic exam and semen that was still inside me was swabbed and collected.

Once the exam was over, a counselor on call for these situations was sent to the room to speak with me. I was given information on rape and a number to call for therapy. Since my mom was on government assistance and Medicaid, I was able to seek counseling for free as a service provided by the hospital. From the hospital an officer took me to the police station and I was placed in a small room with a metal table and two very uncomfortable chairs, one across from the other. The walls, the chairs, the table, the floor, the ceiling, everything appeared to be the same drab grey color. I repeated to the officer everything that had occurred, everything that I had told my mom, everything that I had told the officer who came to our apartment. My story never changed. I was confident in my decision to report the assault and my decision to stand up for myself.

The officer said he spoke with Johnny and said Johnny had a different story. I didn't care. He said he saw the bat in the corner of the kitchen but that Johnny denied threatening me with it. I didn't care. He said Johnny said I liked it and that I agreed to return to see him the next day. Again, I didn't care. I knew it was all lies and I told the officer just that. I didn't care what Johnny said. He RAPED ME!

"Okay, okay. Calm down. You thirsty? Let me get you something to drink." He left the room.

For what seemed like forever, I sat there waiting for the officer to return. I didn't know where my mom was and I wanted more than anything for this to all be over and done with. Maybe I didn't want to go through with pressing charges. Maybe it wasn't worth it. No, it was worth it and I was going to go through with it no matter what. I may not have fought Johnny off like I wanted to but this time, I decided I wouldn't give in.

The officer returned to the room with a soda, sat down and looked me in the eyes and asked, "Was this the first time you had sex? I mean, were you a virgin before this?"

"No." Immediately his body language shifted to a position of less interested after I answered.

"How many boys have you had sex with?"

"Two." I lied.

"Do you realize if this goes to trial it will be your word against his?" He sat back in his chair. "Since you weren't a virgin and because you didn't fight him back like someone who didn't want to have sex, you know it will be hard to prove he raped you?" With that single statement from the officer, the person sworn to serve and protect, I started to care. "Are you sure you want to do this? You have to be sure, you know."

NEVERTHELESS

"I want my mommy," I said. And he motioned for me to leave.

My mom was sitting in another part of the station. I told her everything the office said and she allowed her head to fall. I saw defeat in her face before I had even gotten used to the esteem I was finally beginning to have for myself. If the officer didn't believe me and now my own mother was finding it difficult to stand with me, how could I do this alone? Before I could answer myself, my mom looked at me and said, "Let's go home."

"Mommy?"

"Baby, if you do this, I mean, if you go through with this, then they will take you away from me and put you in a foster home," she said. "The system is going to say I'm unfit and you know if they start investigating, they will find out I'm working and all this trouble is going to come. Please, for me, just drop it. Your mother, Oshun, will take care of him. Don't worry."

She referred to the orisha as my mother. She gave the responsibility of my protection and my defense to the Yoruba deity she believed to be one of the most powerful of all the orishas, and who is depicted as a protector of love, beauty, and femininity. She assured me that Oshun's love for me would undoubtedly bring about the end to Johnny because he brought hurt upon a child who belonged to her. I wanted to believe her. I had to believe her. I needed someone to care enough for me to defend me. I accepted Oshun as a replacement for my mom.

As a child, Jesus wasn't a name used in my home and although I didn't know what to tell people when they found out we weren't Christians, I knew not to tell them about the animal sacrifices and other rituals performed in my home. My mom believed everyone was born under a god and a sign, like astrology and zodiacs. The god she believed ruled over me was Oshun, the god of love, harmony, and sex; how grossly contradictory this seemed. My mom truly believed all she only needed to perform an animal sacrifice, with an offering of alcohol and honey to appease this god and consequently grant us resolution. But I didn't want resolution from a god of harmony. I wanted love, support and protection from my mother.

NEVERTHELESS

When we arrived home, I immediately went to bed. I wanted to close my eyes to the entire day and wake only to find that it was all a horrible nightmare. The room was so dark that night, for which I was grateful. I pulled the blanket up to cover my head and cried as quietly as I could so not to disturb my mom or let on to her how hurt I was that no one was going to stand up for me. No one wanted to hear my truth, no one wanted to say publicly and loudly that what happened to me was wrong. Why did it matter that I wasn't a virgin? I didn't deserve what he did to me.

Just before I drifted off to sleep, my mom came in the room and sat on the edge of the bed. She rested her hand on my arm and said, "I know you're hurt and upset. I wish I could take the pain away but I can't. I still hurt from when it happened to me."

I knew my mom had a rough childhood and a dark story to tell but this would be the first time I realized she had been a victim of sexual abuse. I could hear the hurt in the sound of her voice as she spoke and the torment she still lived as a consequence was also obvious. I held back my disappointment and my tears. Did this mean I too would carry this pain into my adult years, into my years as a parent? Instead of wanting her protection, I found myself wanting to protect her. The comfort I was hoping for and still longed for from her would become secondary.

I had so many questions for the only other person beside the police, the nurses, and counselor who knew what had happened to me. I wanted to know from the person in whom all my hope and trust lived just how to endure this pain. But before I could muster up the words to whisper them from my lips, my mom, as if knowing what I was going to ask her, spoke, "You need to stop crying and wipe your face. You'll get over it. It's just pussy."

Darkness overcame me that night and though I tried to understand what she meant, I only grew angrier and more withdrawn. It wasn't "just pussy" like she said and yet, in a way I wanted it to be. I began working to convince myself that it was "just" that. I learned to separate and detach myself from 'IT' but I didn't realize I was separating myself from love, faith and peace also.

NEVERTHELESS

The charges were dropped and life went on. I never spoke about that night to my mom ever again. But she was wrong, I didn't simply get over it. For years I tried to pretend it didn't happen. I tried to pretend I didn't care that it happened and for years I tried to pretend I wasn't mad that she didn't fight for me. The abuse of that night only added to the pain and shame in my life. I had to escape, but where would I go. Everywhere I went, I was there also.

It would take something great to heal this pain. It would take someone greater than anyone I had ever known to take away the abandonment, the shame, and the chains that had me bound. It would take someone to whom an animal sacrifice was no longer required. Eventually I would come to know the very One who would do all this and more. Many say their lives changed when they 'found' Jesus but the fact is Jesus wasn't lost. We were. My life changed when I found my way to Him. The love that followed revealed purpose and started me on my way to the peace that I longed for.

SHARONDA JONES

Me and my mom at the temple.

7

What could be better than middle school with its clichés and ridicule of all introverted adolescents who failed to exhibit early signs of young adult ostentatiousness? Why, high school of course.

Three years of participating in the dramatic production of me fulfilling the expectation of others included traveling an hour on the metro each way, from home to school and back. All the kids who had tortured and mocked me at Langley Junior High would undoubtedly attend McKinley Tech high school because it shared the same neighborhood block. I was adamant about not going to McKinley. I wanted a fresh start and a new beginning.

When my middle school counselor announced there would be an opportunity for ninth graders to select a school other than the one in their neighborhood, I jumped at the chance. The only requirement was I had to enroll in the focus subject for that school. Each high school in D.C. had a focus subject like communications, international studies, or engineering. I chose Spingarn Senior High for its pre-architecture program.

I excelled in math, and science though art was still my passion. It made sense that I would do well in a program that combined the science, math and that which I loved the most, art. I enrolled the following fall semester and things were beginning to look up. I was hopeful for what was to come. My mom and I were mending our relationship and consistency was returning to our lives as she had been stable in my life for two consecutive years. So I was little caught off guard when I heard the words that I had come to dread, "I have to leave but it won't be long. Be a good girl."

NEVERTHELESS

This time, I was sent to live with the very same woman whose husband had made an advance towards me five years earlier. He had died but assuredly the tension was still there. Her house was located in the Benning Heights area of Southeast D.C. nicknamed 'Simple City', near Benning Road. The metro commute to my new high school wasn't as bad as it was when I lived in Northeast D.C. but I had to walk through a different neighborhood as a new face that stood out. Gangs were common and crime was rampant in this area. Shoes hung from powerlines in excess to reflect the number of lives that had been taken violently and the sounds of gunshots were so common that the sound of silence was far more alarming. My route went through the housing projects known as Benning Terrace. I was supposed to focus on school but I couldn't. I wanted to put my all into the new program but I couldn't. Hopelessness was returning. I was suffocating and had no idea how to get out. This was my life now. I had to accept it.

I met a boy who showed me attention and he was willing to protect me. It wasn't safe to be single girl living in a place like Benning Terrace or any gang-affiliated territory. I was safer with a boyfriend who was in the gang than I was single girl. His family lived in one of the units of the complex and they accepted me immediately. I felt more accepted by them than I had by any of the other people I had lived with. His mom adored me. Their living conditions were basic; they were impoverished like all the other residents in the community. However, money was not an issue simply because of the lifestyle and the illegal means by which my boyfriend generated income. Although we were only 15 years old, his mom allowed me to stay in his room, sleep in his bed and be with him like man and wife, under her roof.

I spent more and more time with them and I loved being there. Her house was always busy, people coming and going, laughing and playing. The candy lady lived in the next court and I enjoyed walking my boyfriend's younger siblings to the window where she conducted her candy affairs. It's amazing how the similarities of my acceptance into the dysfunctional family of my boyfriend mirror the acceptance of my mom by those who inducted her into the West-African religion. The enemy obviously uses the same tricks masked in unimposing disguises.

NEVERTHELESS

When I learned I was pregnant, I was terrified and elated at the same time. I was scared to tell my mom and yet happy because my boyfriend's mom was happy. She had it all worked out, I would get on public assistance, move into their complex and be one happy family. It wasn't necessarily the picture I had painted for my life but I felt it would be insulting for me to tell his mom that the life she lived every day was not the life I wanted for myself. I wanted her love. I wanted her acceptance and I was terrified that her love for me would end if I didn't have the baby. I decided I had to tell my mom. There I was again, sitting down to write my mom a letter to tell her what had transpired in her absence. And once again, my mom responded with a return trip home to deal with me.

My mom was adamant about an abortion. I secretly wanted the abortion as well but I was torn between the fears of being a teen mother and the fear of losing the new family I had gained. I wanted the love of my boyfriend's mom to continue because I had lost hope of receiving love from my own parent. I did not want to receive welfare. I did not want to live in the Benning Terrace housing projects and I did not want to give up my life to motherhood at 15. I still had hope for better.

Interestingly, although I was hurt by my mom's abandonment, her absence created an opportunity for me to wonder about more. I wanted to be, in her sight, a good girl whom she would return to and care for. I wanted her to love me and I knew if I had the baby, she would never forgive me. It wasn't a chance I was willing to take.

When my mom arrived, she already had the abortion appointment scheduled for the next day. I don't think anything could have prepared me for my first trip to the abortion clinic. Yes. I said first trip. It took two trips to the clinic for me to finally go through with the procedure. The first visit was an extremely emotional nightmare.

There were protestors picketing in front of the building, pleading with girls not to commit the sin of killing our babies. They distributed pamphlets with horrible images of mutilated babies and stories of babies having to endure the actual 'feeling' of being aborted. It was unbearable. My mom, exasperated that they were trying to talk me out of having the abortion, yelled back at them, "Will you take care of it then?" Eventually, we were able to navigate through the crowd and into the building but by the time it was my turn to speak with the nurse, I had begun to have second thoughts. Maybe the protestors were right. I couldn't do it. Even with my mom's persistence, threats and anger, because I said no, the nurses were not allowed to proceed any further. Finally, my voice mattered.

I left shortly after arriving, with my mother giving me a stern silent treatment. Since I had not been inside long enough to have had the procedure, the protestors cheered and applauded me as I left. My mom didn't share in their jubilation; she was livid. Later that evening, my mom begged me not to ruin my life this way. She said the baby's spirit would be returned to God and that life would go back to normal. I wasn't sure whose normal she was referring but I knew I couldn't bring a baby into her normal or mine.

A few days later, we returned to the clinic and, with no protestors present, I went through with the abortion. Although the medical procedure was over, the process of dealing with regret, sorrow, shame and sadness over the idea of life discarded stayed with me for years. The constant thinking about my baby and the person he or she would have been, the dreams that followed of a face and the imagined sound of his or her voice still comes to mind even today. The process of an abortion is NEVER over. Only the procedure.

My boyfriend broke up with me because he felt I put my mom before him and his mom. I continued my friendship with his mom long after the breakup and even after her son was shot and killed at the age of 17. She never fully understood why I chose to go through with the abortion rather than emancipating myself to become a teenage mom. Some things a child just shouldn't have to explain.

When my mom left, I thought punishment was over. But it wasn't. She moved me from the godmother's house and the neighborhood of my boyfriend and his mom to the home of another temple member, who was also a priestess in the Yoruba practice. I will just say that it wasn't an ideal situation but it was who my mom chose. I realized later that my mom was convinced to leave me with her out of financial obligation to the priestess. My mom would pay rent for me to live there and in a way, was doing her part to financially support the expenses of the shrine that was also housed there. But as a 15 year old, I had my own ideas and thoughts about the way I wanted to live my life. The life I desired for myself did not include orisha worship, psychic readings, or animal sacrifices.

Shortly after moving into the home of my new caretaker, a trip was planned for us to travel to Sheldon, S.C. for an initiation ceremony. Located in Sheldon is the only African village on American soil, the Oyotunji Village. Residents who call the village home, which includes a king and his royal court, practice as their counterparts do in Ghana and Nigeria. Today, the site takes on tourists who want to experience the authenticity of an African village, but back then, to a 15 year old girl, driving to South Carolina to stay in a village without electricity or running water, for a ceremony that involved face cutting, was hell. I was forced to go, locked in the house and not allowed to go to school to ensure that I would be along for the trip.

After we returned home, I waited until late one evening and I packed a bag and walked out. I had nothing planned other than to leave. I stopped at a payphone to call a girlfriend who lived nearby with her grandmother. She agreed to sneak me in through her basement if I promised to be out before her grandmother woke the next morning. I had to be as quiet as I could to avoid being discovered. Confined to the basement and forced to be silent meant finding alternatives if I had to use the bathroom. She gave me an old coffee can to use and told me to be sure to take it outside with me when I left. The following morning, I did as I was told and secretly left out through the backdoor of the basement, with coffee can in hand. I discarded the contents and threw the can in a neighbor's trash. For almost a week, I went from friend to friend, telling their parents that I had permission to spend the night. No one thought to check.

Eventually the secrecy and underground help would run out. My last resort was a girl that I met in a counseling group for rape and sexual assault victims. I figured who better to ask than someone whose background had as much pain as mine. Not sure if that's sound advice: 'find someone with a problem like yours to get help'. Obviously, if the person has similar problems and haven't found a solution for themselves, then most likely they won't have a viable solution for you either.

She had a cousin who lived with his family in the Congress Heights area of Southeast D.C. She said he could help me if I went to see him. With the understanding that my part of the exchange would include sex, he agreed to help me. We drove to a motel on Branch Avenue in Temple Hills, across from the Iverson Mall, where he paid for a room. We checked in on Saturday and he gave me $10 spending money. He spent the night Saturday and left early Sunday. I used the money to purchase underwear from a store in the mall because I left all my clothes at the last place I stayed. I was thankful to be able to shower and have a change of underwear. I waited for him to return on Sunday with food for me to eat. He returned but he wasn't alone.

At the sound of the key unlocking the door, I perked up because I had grown lonely and bored. But as soon as the door opened, my smile faded. With him were two guys and they brought in a small luggage bag. The two guys sat in the chairs next to the door and the guy I was with sat at the table. I had been trained and around enough drug dealers to know that my eyes were to always look away. I focused intently on the television, praying to God under my breath that my behavior was to their satisfaction. They pull the packages out and began processing the white powder. I could see them peripherally but I knew to never let on that I was paying attention. As I stared at the television pretending to be thoroughly engaged in the program, I could see one of the guys motioning with a slight head nod towards me and I heard him say, "What's up?" The guy I was with responded, "Nah, not her."

In a time when sex trafficking and abuse is rampant, I was spared. In a time when women are forced into prostitution and violence, I was spared. All of them left shortly afterwards and the guy I was with didn't return to spend the night. I slept alone, gladly. Realizing all that I had been protected from, I cried relief into my pillow and fell soundly asleep. The next morning, Monday, he returned to check out. He drove me down Branch Avenue into the city, gave me another $10 bill and said, "See ya." I never saw him again. I boarded a bus on Minnesota Avenue and transferred to Benning Road. My destination, school. While I would love to say I went because I was an aspiring scholar who knew the importance of a quality education, but the only reason was for free breakfast and lunch. Of course, I enjoyed school; the work wasn't challenging, and the teachers were easy to please. It was student life that was arduous.

Another reason I went to school and attended all my classes was because of the comfort of consistency. School was a place where things fit for me. But this Monday was different. As if God wasn't finished answering my prayer, an astute English teacher noticed something wasn't quite right with me, she pulled me aside and asked if I was okay. I admitted everything that had happened to me up to the point where I was standing before her. I told her I was homeless and that I had no place to go. With tears in her eyes, she asked if I wanted to stay with her until things were resolved and I got the help I needed. While I don't suggest that teachers take in children, nor should children agree to live with a teacher but this was exactly what I needed. I can't fathom the risk she took by giving me shelter and yet, without hesitation, she did. She shared my situation with another teacher, and together they took turns providing me with place to stay until other arrangements could be made. Eventually, they arranged for me to receive temporary room and board at the Sasha Bruce House in Northeast D.C. Sasha Bruce Youthworks is an organization that provides shelter for homeless, abandoned, and runaway children for a short period, with the goal of returning the young person to their families. They connected with my mom and she agreed to move back home to provide a safe environment for me to live. After both individual and family counseling, and proof that she had her own place, I left the youth house and moved in with my mom.

My senior year of high school was the best year of all my years of school and yet I could tell my mom was still troubled. Regardless of how badly I wanted to help, I didn't know how to make her pain go away. I had my own pain and yet my issues were secondary while I focused on hers. I resented her for her weakness and I felt like she resented me for making her weak. It was a wretched cycle to be in. Not that

NEVERTHELESS

I made it a goal but I graduated valedictorian of my high school class and voted most likely to succeed. My objective wasn't to prepare my road to college. I didn't dream of prizes, awards, degrees or fortunes. I wanted love. I wanted what seemed to me what everyone else had and didn't appreciate. There were no discussions about college, and teachers assumed the top scholar had her life all planned out. They were wrong.

In my mind, I was enjoying my senior year and yet everyone assumed I wanted more. I didn't see what others saw in me or for me. At the beginning of the school year, a portion of my life as a homeless teen was told to the world by the Children's Defense Fund and the local station for NBC as part of their "Beating the Odds" segment. Instead of inspiring me, it only caused me shame and embarrassment. A moment that should have propelled me onto greatness only catapulted me into deeper fear and isolation.

SHARONDA JONES

Graduation Day
Spingarn Senior High, 1993

NEVERTHELESS

Separation, isolation, and division are weapons of the enemy, whose focus and intention is to steal, kill, and to destroy. Though camouflaged to deceive us into thinking there's something new under the sun, sin is the same today as it was thousands of years ago; different wrappings but the same motives. Until we address one another as brothers, and until we learn to love as God created us to do, then we will continue give room to the ways of the enemy.

I am thankful to God for everyone He has put in my path to show me and to teach me about love, unconditional love, that supersedes racial barriers. In addition to my favorite big sister, I was blessed to have white teachers who were kind and patient with me, doctors, counselors and social workers who treated me as if I mattered regardless of race. As a whole, we would be further along if we didn't have discord about race or beliefs, and the enemy knows this. That's why he simply sits back and throws darts of doubt and deception our way. Like buzzards that swoop down to the carcass on the side of the road, people who are focused on keeping us divided run to social media and videos of fights, death and crime to feed on carcass left by sin of hatred for one another as well as for ourselves.

My high school was all black and was located in a predominantly low-income neighborhood. The adjacent community, known as Langston Terrance, sat directly across from the Langston Golf Course and Driving Range on Benning Road. The golf course, and the community of apartment homes, was named after John Mercer Langston, the first African American to be elected into public office during the Reconstruction period.

NEVERTHELESS

Completed in 1938, the community was the first federally funded public housing project in D.C. and was designed with shared common spaces, a library, outdoor living spaces and play areas for children. When we lived there, which ironically was long before my days of high school, it was still the haven for low-income to middle class blacks who loved and cared for the community in which they lived. Availability was limited as many of the residents stayed until death simply because the affordable rent created a contentment to stay. Opponents to public housing claim it is this contentment that creates a pattern among families living in poverty to only focus on getting into public housing rather than developing a mindset to get out of it.

I remember the first time I faced a major decision and race was used as a deciding factor. All throughout elementary, junior high and high school, most of my learning was done in an environment filled with kids my complexion. When the announcement was made that I would be valedictorian, I still had not made a decision about college. My quandary wasn't deciding which school to attend but rather if I would go at all. To ease the financial burdens of post-secondary education, my counselor decided I would be a perfect applicant for the 21st Century Scholarship at George Washington University.

The head of the university, Stephen Tratensburg, had created a program that offered full scholarships to include room and board, to high achieving scholars of D.C. public high schools who had financial need of assistance. The only issue was that George Washington did not offer architecture as a major, and I had spent the last three years convincing myself and others that this was what I wanted to do with my life.

I turned to one of the teachers who I often turned to for advice. She was one of the two teachers who took me into her home. I trusted her and valued her opinion because I had never considered college or what I would do after high school. My mom worked jobs off-the-books because she received welfare. College wasn't something I considered to be for me. I would graduate from high school and get a job. My family needed money and I didn't understand how college fit into that equation.

At that time, as a child living in poverty and uncertain about tomorrow, I didn't have the words of

NEVERTHELESS

the first African-American First Lady of the United States, Michelle Obama telling me, "Don't be afraid. Be focused. Be determined. Be hopeful. Be empowered. Empower yourselves with a good education, then get out there and use that education to build a country worthy of your boundless promise." Of course, we had role models and leaders whom we heard about, read about and even wrote about every February but these weren't people in my neighborhood that I connected with. Instead, my high school had a daycare and rather than teaching kids how to type or open a bank account, classmates learned hands on how to care for the babies they brought with them to school.

When the offer to go to George Washington University came, I listened to the teacher's advice over the counselor who convinced me to apply. "Don't go to George Washington. They only want you because you're black and they have a quota to fill." Right then I got a reality check that there would be times when my race would be used for the gain of someone else. I was told that it wasn't about me, it was about them. And I believed it. Something positive was made negative and I didn't understand how to process it.

But it was about me. In fact, it should have only been about me but others made it about them. My decision was being framed around the issues that others had with me going to a predominantly white school and their racial biases. The adults decided I needed other options so I applied and was accepted to attend Shaw University and North Carolina A&T State University. Despite no financial assistance offered by either, I was told I belonged with people like me, which meant the same skin color, even if it meant taking on student loans, struggling to finance enrollment or leaving home with no family support. I turned down the scholarship and left for N.C. A&T that fall.

The fact that there are many programs and institutions willing to help students who struggle with very grown up issues by offering scholarships and financial support is inspiring. However, there should be a component to accompany the financial assistance that deals with developing coping skills. Depending on the challenges a young person has experienced and the ability or lack thereof for those in their lives to offer proper guidance, financial support may not be all the person needs. For an organization to give a child a monetary award, then pat them on the back and never see them again is not as helpful as giving them guidance through the process. It is the extra step of directing and mentoring them until they are able to stand on their own that should be offered as well. Too often we expect telling our youth they are amazing is enough or telling them how we walked ten miles to school with no shoes, picking cotton along the way should encourage them to do better. Guess what, it doesn't.

Countless children are being discarded and overlooked simply because guidance is lacking. The "each one teach one" movement has been lost on younger generations because many people are trying to "get theirs" with no concern for others being lifted in the process. We have to get beyond the point of simply giving a donation or a seed without hanging around long enough to see if the need was met or if the seed we sowed was received.

While not every dollar donated or article of clothing collected will allow for verifying receipt but we can do more on a larger scale. Children need mentors and life-coaches. Children need more than a dollar to buy a few books, they need someone to show them what else is available to them and encouragement to stay on track. At-risk, emotionally damaged children, like the child I used to be, require so much more than a pat on the back or the instruction, "be a good girl, okay." They need our stories of overcoming the obstacles they will most certainly face.

As a recipient of the Children's Defense Fund 'Beat the Odds' award, I received a plaque that reads "Dear Lord be good to me the sea is so wide and my boat is so small", a laptop computer, and a savings bond. I pawned the laptop and tried to cash in the savings bond but it hadn't matured enough.

The awards dinner was attended by the newly elected President Bill Clinton and Mrs. Hillary Clinton. Additional speakers that year were the acclaimed poet, author and civil rights activist Maya Angelou, and former Essence editor-in-chief Susan Taylor who introduced me at the dinner. I remember thinking how absolutely beautiful Ms. Taylor was with her signature braids and how honored I was that she knew my name and my story. I never connected

NEVERTHELESS

who she is with the person I had the potential to become.

As the guest speaker for the program, Mrs. Clinton spoke my name and the names of the other recipients when she called us extraordinary, having "high hopes" for us because we "demonstrated the indomitable will of the human spirit to overcome and beat the odds". As she spoke, none of this actually registered with me about me. I was more intrigued by the stories of the other recipients and felt they had beaten the odds far more than I had. I had merely lived life in a way that was unavoidable. I survived, I felt, by default. I didn't see my ability to endure as something that I intentionally planned or purposed. It wasn't until I began to tell others my story that I began to think perhaps, my life wasn't that normal.

She went on to say, "So clearly is how with a helping hand, with a listening ear, with a chance that is given to another to make a good decision for that person's life, there is always hope. [We must] "recognize that we owe our children more than we have been giving to them. And we need to begin paying that to them in the ways that count for children – with love and attention, the right mixture of discipline and caring, with schools that work, with neighborhoods that are safe, with health care that is available, with role models that encourage young people to dream dreams and believe they too can lead productive lives."

I believe this was why my teacher encouraged me to go to the historically black university, N.C. A&T, over George Washington University. She believed I would get the support I needed, encouragement and mentoring from the black community rather than just the financial support to pay for college. But what I needed, our community didn't generally welcome or encourage; I needed counseling and guidance about life, not just the college experience. Leaving high school meant leaving what had sustained me and what I had come to rely on. My teachers were an extension of home, similar to surrogates, and they wanted more for me than I understood to want for myself.

Children who grow up in poverty or with extreme lack are forced to suppress emotions and thoughts that most don't realize children experience. Coupled with lack of confidence in self-expression or the inability to voice their pain, anger suppression and emotional issues can lead to poor decision making, and social and emotional management issues. Commonly disregarded in black communities, counseling and mental health management is stigmatized as a tool only for the severely insane.

"You're crazy" or "you're lunching" (which denotes being 'out to lunch' in one's mind) were common phrases when I tried to express myself to others. No one I knew personally received treatment from a therapist. My mom allowed me to see a counselor after the sexual assault but that was only because social services required it. When I was a child, my mom could not afford to make mental health and counseling part of my normal care management. As an adult, I couldn't afford not to.

Later, I would understand the importance that counseling has in my Christian walk as well as the importance of my Christian walk in counseling. For as long as I received counseling without mention of my faith or the measure of my faith, I would always need counseling. But once I began to work on my faith, learning who and whose I am in Christ, I can see how my faith equips me to move from the counselee to the counselor. Not because I have all the answers but because I know God's Word does, and it is His Word that equips us with the ability to help others. There will be times when it is necessary to stand up for our unique accomplishments as a race but when we put other down to promote our own, then we are standing in vain. When we deny the rights of others or turn down the help we need simply because of past hurt, then we are standing in vain. The enemy wants you and I to focus only on the 'standing' part of standing in vain, without acknowledging what is contributing to the struggle rather than alleviating it. When we choose not to love, choose not to trust God for our interactions with one another, when we turn our backs to those in need simply because of the color of their skin, then we are like buzzards circling over the slowly dying.

Allow love to penetrate moments you encounter and situations where you cannot conceive on your own what you should do. Don't allow hatred to have any place in your life and even when others around you are giving into to temptation to participate in negativity, take a stand that is NOT in vain. Choose life, the life that Christ Jesus came, died and was risen for you to have.

NEVERTHELESS

Wake from a slumber of doubt and insecurity; wake from the series of behaviors that are based on the pains of the past. Allow God's love to free you from repeating cycles of hurt, abuse, and unforgiveness before they become fixed in your mind's picture of yourself. Allow your dreams to help shape who you will become rather than remind you of the hurt you used to live.

Beat the Odds

Children's Defense Fund
1992 Annual Benefit

Wednesday, November 18, 1992

Pension Building
National Building Museum
Judiciary Square
Washington, DC

**USE ENTRANCE ON G STREET
AT 4TH STREET, NW**
*PLEASE NOTE THAT THIS ENTRANCE
IS DIFFERENT FROM LAST YEAR*

VIP Cocktails 6:00 p.m.
Dinner and Awards Ceremony 7:30 p.m.

Please arrive promptly at
6:00 p.m. to allow for
possible security procedures

Business attire
Valet Parking
ADMIT ONE

BELIEVE

*"Hatred paralyzes life; love releases it.
Hatred confuses life; love harmonizes it.
Hatred darkens life; love illuminates it."*

–DR. MARTIN LUTHER KING, JR.

9

How often do you laugh? Are you a naturally funny person or someone who has to work hard to force the corners of your mouth upward? Do you intentionally seek out happiness and humor?

I do, now. Too often we settle for stumbling upon moments of joy and laughter rather than purposely seeking them. Seeking, which means pursuing with a greater purpose and intensity than to merely look over, is something I believe is lost on the males in my family. I used to joke that they only look for things with their eyes. When I look for something, I use my hands to move things around and uncover what is hidden. Instead, they simply walk into a room or the place where they last remembered the item being, look around, and walk away without finding it. Then I would follow their same steps, move some things around and behold – whatever they were looking for, there it was!

It got to the point where I would stand idly by waiting for their failed attempt before making my own attempt of finding what was lost. I felt it was important to at least allow them the opportunity of success before swooping in and saving the day with my superwoman cape. Rather than having them get used to me doing the work, I wanted them to get tired of my heroics. The results of this approach are still pending because there are times when I know they are purposely not looking as hard as they could, counting on me to come to their rescue. Then there are times when they go overboard in their search and eventually find whatever it is they're looking for to avoid the mom/wife domination that was inevitable. Oh well, a victory is a victory however it comes.

NEVERTHELESS

Being funny or having moments where I laugh and enjoy myself is now something that I look forward to. Laughing reminds me of the time when I was a little girl and I used to put on a one-girl show for my mom. I would pretend to be multiple characters, using pillow cases, towels, or sheets to create the different looks of the characters. I loved to hear her laugh and her smile was so beautiful to me. It still is, even with the winkles of life that have formed around her face as signs of all that she has been through and overcome. Once we moved to D.C., I tried everything in my little girl ability to bring back the happiness of Charlotte but it wasn't enough. She would laugh for a little while, give me a hug and then she'd leave.

For years, I continued to seek the same comfort that I felt through laughter. But that type of comfort comes from a Godly revelation of joy and peace. I wanted to replace the joy I felt in Charlotte but growing up in D.C. was proving too difficult to ever again have the joy I remembered. I had to learn to harden my expressions so no one would think I was a pushover or weak. It was important to appear as if you could handle yourself in any situation, even if it was far from the truth. Classmates in high school and college would say they thought I was unapproachable. "Good," I thought. The flipside is that regardless of how much I tried to portray a rough and tough exterior, the kind, gentle and considerate person God created me to be was still there waiting to come out and shine bright. There would be times when I couldn't contain it and the silly side of me would show. Except I didn't have the confidence to back it up. I didn't understand that I could be fun and confident, laugh and still be taken seriously. Laughter to me was a sign of weakness and vulnerable was what I wanted to avoid.

It wasn't until my final years high school when the struggle of masking the person I was with the face I wanted the world to see became too great. My teachers wanted me to be the scholar but I wanted to be liked by my peers. Classmates thought I was too nerdy to be cool and at home my mom was too busy with her own life to understand the peer and social pressures I was under. I had to pretend everything was wonderful everywhere I went. Otherwise, I would be accused of simply being moody. No one wanted to hear I was sad or depressed. My mom's response when I shared my feelings of sadness with her was "so am

NEVERTHELESS

I." I had to deal with my feelings the best way I could. I decided it was best for me to be alone. Unfortunately, in the company of one, I was resigned to believing being me meant being rejected and unacceptable to be around. Being me meant I had to be alone. Otherwise I had to be someone else. Anyone but me. I struggled with this lack of self-acceptance all through high school and although I hoped things would be different when I left for college, my issues had their bags packed and ready to go to college with me.

When I first arrived on the campus of N.C. A&T, a mix of emotions overwhelmed me. I was terrified, nervous and anxious as I arrived for freshmen orientation, but I was also hopeful and full of anticipation simply because it was all so very new and different. I started to hope again. Although I had not technically returned to my birthplace of Charlotte, I was in Greensboro which was close enough. I was happy to be back in North Carolina and no longer in D.C. I was able to start new and create the "me" I wanted to be. Then it dawned on me that I was the only freshman at student orientation without a parent or guardian.

SHARONDA JONES

Before I left for school I had begun the process of detaching myself from the emotional disappointments surrounding my mom but there hadn't been enough time to avoid feeling the shame of being the only out-of-state new student there alone. Thankfully, that night I met the young ladies who would become my family away from home. We were all from out of town and from different walks of life. Even though still relatively young, we all had unique and adventurous stories to tell. My life was no longer so outlandish, which created among our group a no-judgement zone. It was exactly what I had longed for. A family.

For the year and a half that I attended N.C. A&T, I saw myself independent of my mom and my childhood. I was my own person, and I loved being able to make my own choices about where I went, who I spoke to and what I did. The irony of being away from home all alone was that the same independence I coveted would become the same isolation that I feared. But for now, I was happy. I was experiencing all that being away at school had to offer. Immediately, I made friends and within a few weeks we already had our posse formed. I bonded with a girl from Pennsylvania who had the funniest accent

NEVERTHELESS

I'd ever heard. She was there on an Army scholarship and also ran track. I was there on a wish and a prayer, and participated in absolutely no extracurricular activities. My extracurricular activities were going to work as a sandwich artist at Subway and trying to find a way to pay for books each semester. We became college besties, or BFFs.

There were three others in our group, two from North Carolina and one from New York. Choosing to go away to school meant leaving my best friends back in D.C. so I was happy to establish new friendships and even happier to start over with people who never knew the old me. I laughed and I loved laughing. I loved caring for these girls and I felt loved by them. And because I loved them, I was ready to fight for them.

We were all majoring in different disciplines and rarely had classes together. During class was the only time during the day that we were not together. Otherwise, we did everything as a unit. When one started dating a guy, the guy had to have a friend for one of us to date as well. Like I said, we were a unit. That was the first year. My second year brought me face to face with some old demons that, as it turns out, I wasn't equipped to handle. While I was prepared to stand up for my friends, I learned that I still wasn't ready to stand up for myself.

In 1993, social media wasn't like it is today, so bullying was done more direct and in person. My bestie began seeing a boy who drove a nice car and was all about his ride. Unfortunately, he was also an abusive person who had a mean streak that caused him to lash out. I didn't care for him but she did, so I had to tolerate him. One night though, he had gone too far and I decided to get back at him through his beloved vehicle. I know, it wasn't my fight and yet I made it mine. I was angry for the way he mistreated her but it wasn't right for me to commit vandalism. My roommate tried to take the blame for me but I refused to let her and took ownership of my actions. She did however help me pay for the damages I caused to his car and we considered everything would go back to normal. She and I considered the matter over. Unfortunately, he didn't feel the same way.

A few days later, while walking across the main campus, I noticed a number of people pointing at me and then turning away when my eyes caught their stare. I tried to ignore it. When I got to class I heard more people whispering and again I tried to ignore it. Later that afternoon, it was time to meet my girlfriends in the cafeteria for an early dinner. But before we could get to the cafeteria, one of the girls in our group ran up to me visibly upset and handed me a sheet of paper that appeared to be a flyer. As soon as I read it, I knew why everyone had been staring at me all day. With a picture of my face, the message below read, "STAY AWAY FROM HER. SHE HAS HERPES." She had gotten the flyer from her boyfriend who had taken it off a wall in the boys' dormitory. I stood frozen in place. I knew exactly where the picture had come from. When my bestie started dating her boyfriend, I started seeing his friend so we could double date. We talked for a little while but he eventually left school because of financial aid issues.

I thought *this couldn't be. Why would someone do this, say THIS?* I had to see it for myself so instead of going to the cafeteria, I headed straight for the boys' dorm. There they were, lining the walls of the hallway, my face and those words. As I began ripping the flyers from the wall, I could hear guys saying, "Man, that's her. That's the girl in the picture."

Everywhere I went the same scene occurred, pointing, whispering and staring. I tried to ignore it but it was getting harder and harder. On campus, no one approached me, but when I attended functions off campus, I was fair game for worse treatment. Sitting in the stands during football games, I was teased. At parties, I was teased. Walking to the grocery store, I was teased. I reported him and although the flyers he made to punish me had come down, the damage was done.

My friends tried their best to take up for me when they were approached or warned to stay away from me, but I didn't want them fighting my battle. I didn't want them to put themselves in receipt of his anger. He decided I deserved this punishment because of the damaged I caused to his car, and there were others who agreed with him. But he never mentioned that the abuse he caused my friend nor did he mention that he received four new tires as a result.

His attack on me was worse than anything I did to his car and he knew it. He felt validated in his actions and there's nothing worse than an assailant who has the support of those around him to continue his assault. But not just validation, he appeared to enjoy ruining my life. I thought it would never end. But even worse than that, I began to believe I deserved it. I started to see how my actions brought about his rage. I began to take ownership of his hatred and justify his actions by my actions. I began to feel as if I owed him more than the reparations I had already paid. Though the damage I caused was material, I began to accept his demand for the sacrifice of my emotional value and my self-worth. I felt helpless and alone. But I had also felt this way five years before in that basement apartment.

While in the moment as a victim, I could only see as far as dealing with the pain in front of me. I wanted to have control but unfortunately, I took ownership of guilt instead. Not having control in both the basement assault and the college bullying incident caused me to take ownership of guilt and defeat. But it wasn't mine to own or control. Satan wanted me to believe it was my fault and that I deserved what was happening to me. But no one deserves to be bullied, assaulted, raped, or abused. No one.

In society, retaliation is a given and people are put to death as punishment for their actions. Men and women stand as judges over other men and women. It is the law of the land. Therefore, there will always be people who believe they have the right to determine and enforce judgement on others. Which is why joy and peace of God are so very important to have. God's joy and peace isn't something the world can give or take away. Regardless of what happens to us or around us, the ability to stand strong, unwavering and unmovable comes from God's love. God is our fortress, our strength and our habitation. No evil is more powerful than our God. But the only way to experience that confidence is with a relationship with Him through Holy Spirit, which at that time, I did not have.

I dreaded going everywhere. Instead of going to class, I would sit confined in my dorm room, contemplating what my next steps should be. My grades eventually reflected my spotty class attendance and I stopped participating in social events on and off campus. Because I felt I deserved it, I decided there was no reason to fight back. I had accepted my fate and had given in. I felt I had gone back in time and was once again sitting on the floor of that small kitchen, looking up into hate filled eyes and longing for someone to come in and save me. No one came. It was all up to me. The only thing I knew to do was walk away. It was what my mom did, it was what she told me to do after the rape, so it would be my solution for this situation as well. He had won. My rapist had won. The man who my mom made more important than me had won. Everyone, I thought, was a winner except me. I was never meant to win or to be happy, to smile or to laugh. Although home was plagued with its problems, I began to long for it and the familiarity of it. The pain from home, a place that I knew, was of more comfort than the pain I felt in this strange land.

Since my grades had dropped significantly, and I no longer had the strength to ignore the social damage that was done, I made the decision to withdraw from all my classes rather than to take a failing grade. I told my advisor that I would return the following Spring semester and make up the classes but I knew I would never come back. I could barely afford to attend A&T and my job at Subway didn't put a dent in the $12k a year tuition that I alone was responsible for paying. Everything fell on my shoulders, on my 19-year-old shoulders and the weight became too much for me to endure by my own strength.

While there are situations when a person being bullied should leave and times to stay and fight, it must be understood that leaving or staying must be done from a position of confidence and certainty. Until a victim of bullying understands that the power a bully has is power that comes from the victim, then they will remain under a bully's control. Anytime there's physical assault or attack, the most important thing is to seek safety, which may mean walking or running away, but find strength in retreating just the same. It is important not to see physically saving yourself as a moment of weakness.

In fact, taking care to avoid destruction is powerful.

A bully who is dangerous enough to attack a person physically is not someone a victim should try to handle alone. In **every** instance of bullying, physical or non-physical, it is important to seek professional help and protection.

NEVERTHELESS

I didn't know it at the time but I could have shut my bully down simply by changing my reaction and response to him. Because of fear and shame, I allowed him to hold me hostage. Freedom was hidden from me. I was held hostage by my insecurity and embarrassment over choosing to leave. I thought I had failed again. But I didn't fail. I left. There's a difference. Sometimes the strength we must exert is in the *leaving* rather than in the *staying*. The fear lies in our view of starting over. It can be seen as scary or it can be seen as exhilarating and fulfilling. It all depends on the perspective of the person starting over. If the ways of this world, to which we should NOT be conformed, had rule over us, then we'd all be distracted with fighting every battle that comes before us. We would be exhausted, weary and not have a mind of peace. Our focus would always be on winning rather than on standing on the already finished work of victory.

Deciding to leave school and return home wasn't easy. I knew there would be questions from those who were happy for me and rumors started by those who were envious. I was embarrassed to say a bully ran me away. So instead I used the excuse that those who knew me would believe. I said I couldn't afford to stay. There was some truth to that excuse, but I never let on to the rest of the story. Until today. There I was valedictorian of my graduating class, who turned down a full scholarship to George Washington University, now a college dropout because of bullying. It seemed like a repulsive picture regardless of the medium I used to present it. Perhaps there is some truth to what Karen D. Arnold wrote in her book, *Lives of Promise: What Becomes of High School Valedictorians*, where she stated [Valedictorians have] "never been devoted to a single area in which they can put all their passion. They obey rules, work hard, and like learning, but they're not the mold-breakers. They work best within the system and aren't likely to change it."

Basically, she said I am great at getting along and not willing to stand out. But what was wrong with fitting in? Everything! God didn't make me to fit in. And yet that's what I wanted to do so badly. I wanted to fit in to the point of disappearing. Except, I was made for love, to laugh, to have joy and peace. And unfortunately for me, I constantly fought becoming who God created me to be.

NEVERTHELESS

The regret of my decision to leave N.C. A&T at the end of 1994 began to have power over me. But God knew how to deal with me. He placed people in my life who would minister just the right words and direct me to my purpose. The following semester, I transferred my credits and my Citizen's Bank scholarship to the University of D.C., where I majored in architectural engineering and architecture. Although my time at N.C. A&T was short, I was blessed to have met Elijah and Marilyn Thorne. After seeing my story of beating the odds and my struggle to pay for school aired on NBC4 Washington, the D.C. chapter of N.C. A&T's alumni association contacted the news station and asked to be connected with me. For the second half of my freshman year and the summer that followed, the chapter's members treated me with such great Aggie love. When I decided to leave A&T, I expected the affection and care they had shown me to end. Almost all of it did. The exceptions were Elijah and Marilyn. They never left my life. Unofficially, they adopted me as their 4th daughter and are still in my life today.

I went on to graduate from the University of D.C. with both an associate's degree in architectural engineering and a bachelor of architecture. Choosing to fight through pain, rejection and embarrassment brought my laugh back. Accomplishing the dream of graduating college helped me to see that I am stronger than I realized. Despite turning down a full scholarship, despite withdrawing from N.C. A&T, despite having a son when I was 20, I was a college graduate and with honors at that!

In my graduation picture, I have the biggest smile and although everyone was smiling that day, I knew I had a lot to be happy for.

A close friend once said I had missed my calling in life and that I should have been a comedian. I found this, in itself, hilarious because I knew my past. She didn't. *If she only knew*, I thought, *she'd know nothing about me was funny*. At least I didn't think so at the time. I've simply had some funny moments and some not-so-funny moments that I choose to laugh at. Like the time in Jamaica, I overheard a conversation between two people where the tourist said to the local tour guide, "You should visit the States."

The guide said, "O yah mon, I no getta visa."

NEVERTHELESS

I interrupted, "You should try getting an American Express. It's easier to get one of those."

I was actually being very serious. Everyone just stared at me.

Then I started looking back over my life in spite of all that I've endured and instead of only seeing the pain of my past, I saw how far God has brought me. I reflected on how my life is filled with joy, and the fact that someone who knew nothing about my past thought I was funny. It brought a smile to my face. How amazing is that? I still had happiness. I actually had the ability to laugh and to make others laugh. The enemy did not succeed in taking my joy away from me. I won and I'm still winning. My faith secures my access to the promises of God through Christ Jesus. And the same is true for you too. When you think about the good in your life in spite of the trouble, you are standing in victory. When you are able to see blessings when everything around you seems to be cursed, you are standing in victory. When you are able to laugh out with a fullness of joy because you understand each new day comes with new mercies, you my friend are standing in victory. So laugh hard. Laugh loud. Laugh like it is a gift that you have to give the world; because it is.

Laughter is believed to instantly cause a reduction in stress and raise the production of serotonin and endorphins, which can ultimately improve the function of the immune system. I am amazed by the power of something so simple, and the only explanation one can give to the source or creation of that power is that it comes from God. I am grateful that He has blessed my family with this gift. I am humbled by the blessings that have manifested in my life through the power of laughter because I didn't grow up laughing. The same generational chains of bondage over my mom's life, over my life, was seeking after the lives of my children and their children too if I didn't confront and rebuke it. I was created to love and to help others realize and experience the joy they have inside through laughter.

The enemy sought to silence my laughter before I would come to know it as a gift that has been already given to me, fully and completely. My love exists to give encouragement and refreshment (Philemon 1:7) but this would have escaped me if the enemy had his way. Only Holy Spirit can fully replace what is missing in the spirit of man (Romans 14:17) and only in knowing and growing in relationship with Holy Spirit will I experience the righteousness, peace and joy of the Kingdom of God. All that my life holds for the glory of God through Christ Jesus would have been lost if I never learned to laugh. All the joy I have to share and the ability to smile from the heart would have gone to the enemy had I not allowed Holy Spirit to fill me with power. This power, I would inevitably learn to use to break the generational chains that wanted to bind me, my seed and my purpose.

Blessedly, in Christ, I learned to have joy, hope and peace. In Christ, I learned to love. In Christ, I learned to laugh. In Christ, I learned that I am called, nevertheless. Nevertheless, I am REDEEMED.

The day NBC4 Washington and Citizen's Bank of Washington surprised me with a scholarship. Not sure how they were able to keep it a secret from me when the entire city knew about it.

10

I believe there is no such thing as coincidence for the born-again believer. It is important not to fall into the trap of witchcraft by believing in luck, coincidence, and happenstance forms any part of our lives. Of course, I may not have the answer to all things but I do have the One who is the answer to all things living on the inside of me. (Galatians 2:20)

All too often believers will say, "something told me...", "luckily, I...", "good luck with...", or my least favorite, "if it wasn't for bad luck, I'd have no luck at all". Even with the Word of God providing all truth, believers continue to revert to tradition and the familiarity of explaining uncertainty as something that's out of God's control. Though this way of speaking and thinking is common and seemingly innocent, it should be considered unacceptable for a believer. What we say is as powerful as what we do because it is the power of our words that shape our lives, and is the same power as Our Father used to shape our universe. Ask me why blessings are overtaking me and I'll answer, "Because I said so." It is important to speak the Word over every situation in your life. And if anyone asks why that which you spoke came to pass, answer them with, "Because I said so."

Before accepting Christ, I know God was still orchestrating and directing me on a path to Him. Every time someone extended their hand to me during a hardship, that was God loving me. Every time a door opened to grant me an opportunity or one closed to keep me from taking a wrong turn, that was God directing me. His love is not just for the righteous. His love is for all of us.

"I will lead the blind by a way they did not know; I will lead them in paths they have not

known. I will make darkness light before them and crooked places straight. These things I will do for them, and not forsake them."

Isaiah 42:16

Newsflash! Even after I accepted Jesus as Lord over my life, I still faced trials and tribulations. In fact, some of the most arduous periods of my life actually happened after I became a Christian. Yet, since becoming a Christian, my life has been the most fulfilled. It's as if before salvation, the enemy saw my soul as something easy to get. But once it was no longer on the auction block, he decided to go for my testimony. It is our testimonies that will help to lead others to Christ, not just our declarations. Allowing the enemy to have my life meant living a life filled with fear until the day of eternal damnation. But by giving my life to Christ, I took that away from the devil. His only recourse was to go after my testimony and my witness.

Every time I proclaim the Good News of Jesus, I'm telling the devil he can't have my testimony. Every time I show the love of the Lord to another, I'm telling him he is a defeated foe. Every time I proclaim the Lord is my strength, my song and my salvation, I am reminding the enemy that my testimony is unto God in Heaven. And with this book, I offer my life and my story as a witnessing tool about the peace of God, my Father, that is available to all who believe and accept Jesus Christ as Lord.

For a believer, there are no coincidences, only submission to God's Word. We can find comfort and assurance in the process of acknowledging Him, trusting Him, and believing He will not only direct our paths, but also lead us back onto the paths of righteousness when we deviate from His plan for our lives. The enemy wants to construe our thinking to the point of being convinced that our plight and predicament is too great for God's forgiveness. This is SUCH A LIE! Nothing is too big or too great for God's love. As believers, it is our responsibility to develop our eyes and ears to see and hear what are tricks of the enemy, and the only way to do this is to know God's Word.

In 1995, as if leaving N.C. A&T wasn't enough for people to count me out of the race, I did something else that would surely serve as a deal breaker for some. After I had transferred to the University of

NEVERTHELESS

D.C., I learned I was pregnant and I decided to keep the baby. It was my sophomore year and financing my independence proved to be harder than I had imagined. But regardless of how difficult it seemed or the detour it caused in my life, it did not discount me from the promised blessings given to me by the grace of God through Christ Jesus.

Becoming a mom meant growing up fast. I was unemployed at the time and was supported by my scholarship and supplemental student loans. I had no idea how I would take care of a baby and eventually everything began to feel as if life was swallowing me whole; if I didn't reach for a life line, then both my baby and I would perish. I'm sure the enemy was pretty pleased with himself at that moment. Many people who were close to me thought, *now she's pregnant, she's going to drop out of school completely and end up just like her momma.* However, rather than being counted out, becoming a mother helped to soften my heart and eventually positioned me to receive a greater love.

In February of the following year, I welcomed a baby boy into the world. I named him Donaven. Within the same year, I also accepted Christ as Lord over my life. When I think about the times during my life that I wanted to give in or when it seemed like the enemy had taken something away from me, the phrase from a popular insurance commercial comes to mind and I imagine myself saying to the devil, "Ahhh devil, you gotta be quicker than that!"

I'm not sure if you've noticed yet, but not much that happens to me is without some fanfare. The day I accepted Jesus as Lord is no exception and I'm sure not many can say their moment with Holy Spirit came while in the process of planning a physical altercation at a church. The guy I was dating at the time was a preacher's kid and his entire family was against us dating because I had a baby out of wedlock. They told him they wanted the best for him and what was best wasn't me. Whenever I called the house, his sister would be extremely rude and often times conveniently forget to give him my messages. Adding insult to injury for them was that he took to my son as if he was my son's father. We started dating while I was pregnant and stayed together until my son was around 3 years old. He did everything for Donaven like a father would do for his child. They hated this. I never understood how a man so loving and kind could come from a home filled with such hatred. I decided enough was enough and with the help of my bestfriend Vee and her cousin, I would confront her on her turf, in front of her family, at their church. Knowing all his family would be attending their weeknight revival, Vee, her cousin and I met at the church. We waited in the car, passed around a marijuana joint and talked about how we were going to get the girl when she came out. It was crazy. I'm not sure what exactly we were going to do but whatever it was, the marijuana aided our preparation.

The night turned out to be less of a spectacle than what we had played out in our minds while we sat in the car. Instead, after getting restless with waiting for the girl to come outside, we went inside the church to try to make her uncomfortable. But it wasn't the girl who was affected. It was me who Holy Spirit began to convict. When nothing transpired and the evening turned out to be a bust, Vee and her cousin left. I stayed behind. The more I listened to the sermon, the less I focused on the issues I had with the sister. My soul began to stir more than it had ever before but out of fear, I left. The following Sunday, I returned to the church and in front of the same people who I had just days before planned to fight, I stood up, walked down the aisle to the altar. In the midst of a lukewarm almost cold reception, I accepted Jesus Christ as Lord. I now had a reason for why I didn't feel right doing the things I was doing, why I didn't fit with the people I was hanging with, and why I had survived it all up to that point in my life; because I was loved enough to die for, blessed enough to be delivered, and strong enough to love in spite of. The day I accepted Jesus into my life was the beginning of a new journey and from that point I was to lean to God instead of my own understanding, except no one told me that part. I allowed Him in but I didn't understand the difference between in my life and over my life.

Shortly afterward, I started working full-time for the United Way of the National Capital Area where I was surrounded by people with a desire to serve. Their work was not just for a paycheck, which is a truth that most people who work for a non-profit organization would affirm. The goal was to make a difference while making a living. Most of them worked long hours, volunteered countless hours to other agencies, and contributed a percentage of their

NEVERTHELESS

salary to an organization of their choosing. The department I worked for was responsible for the campaign advertisements and media productions that were often used locally for television commercials and solicitations. We also planned and executed the quarterly campaign luncheons that highlighted the progress and successful completion of the local campaigns in Maryland, D.C. and Northern Virginia.

One day as I was leaving for the evening, the receptionist asked of my plans for the weekend. Usually my weekends were used to catch up on my rest after working during the day and going to school at night, every night, and some Saturday mornings. I said I didn't have any plans. She replied, "Not even church?"

I almost felt, in that moment, as if my life was empty despite all that was on my plate. I was a single mother, a fulltime student and a fulltime employee, but since I didn't have plans for church, I thought she considered me a slacker. Not since I accepted Christ had I been back to church. I told her no and then she reached into her purse and handed me a flyer that she said she had received in the mail earlier that week. It was an invitation to attend church service at Spirit of Faith Christian Center in Temple Hills, MD. She said she already had a church home and handed me the card.

It was April 1999 when I attended my first service at Spirit of Faith Christian Center, with my son by my side. It was where I needed to be to grow my faith, to hear the Word of God, to learn whose I am. I joined the following Sunday and have been a partner since. I wish I could say nothing else bad happened to me from that point on, but I can't. In fact, greater pressures seemed to come my way but this time the trials I came against were viewed from a different perspective. I embodied the attitude that whatever else was to come, I had everything I needed to handle it. I found an overwhelming comfort in that fact that as a Christian, I now have a road map, a guidebook, or how-to manual and better than that, a role model to serve as my mentor. I was no longer alone and what I had gone through and would go through in the future would never be able to put me back where I once was.

NEVERTHELESS

Practically with every obstacle that appeared in my life, as if designed to take me completely out of the race of life, God had already provided a way of escape. Around the same time that I joined Spirit of Faith and began growing under the Word, my mom who was watching my son both day and night so I could work and go to school, decided she no longer wanted to keep him at the rate I was paying her. I was devastated. I couldn't afford more than I was already giving her. This was nothing but an attempt of the enemy to distract me, to cause me to focus on what I was losing. Nevertheless, as the enemy was trying to cause me to throw in the towel, God had already provided a way. For a second time, my godmother's mother, Grandma Toots, offered to help my family. The first offer was to my mom when she needed someone to care for me and the second offer was now to me to take care of Donaven. I didn't realize it at the time but that was the first adoption in my family. She adopted us.

By 2000, my esteem had grown; I was surrounded by loving people and was growing in God's Word. While I began to see my worth and wanted more from my relationship with the preacher's kid, he wasn't able meet the needs that I began to develop as a woman of virtue. Now, I wanted to be married. I wanted what I thought, foolishly, every other church going woman had. I wanted to be an "honest woman". He, on the other hand, began cheating with a woman who attended his church, with his family's approval of course.

The breakup was hard on me because it brought back many of the insecurities that I thought I had conquered. Instead of conquering them, I had simply avoided thinking about them. I was distracted in my relationship, distracted with being a full-time student and distracted with motherhood. I was busy trying to pretend I had it all, that I was biblical and holy.

To fill the void left by another failed relationship, I decided to serve as a big sister in the Big Brother Big Sister program. Having been a little sister in the program before, I knew the impact and the benefit a person can bring to a child who needs a role model and emotional support from an adult. I could tell love was beginning to shape my life because of how my life was changing and the fact that I wanted to be a blessing of love to another person. Because I was

NEVERTHELESS

under the Word of God regularly, I grew in the things of God. Unfortunately, there's a false sense of security that comes from hearing the Word only and not really having revelation of its power and authority. The enemy knows a new believer can experience this, as was in my case. I was on the right track by giving back but I wasn't prepared when it opened the door to a skilled manipulator.

I was matched as the big sister to a beautiful, smart and confident 12 year old who was confined to a wheelchair because of cerebral palsy. No one would have ever thought she was handicap by her mental sharpness, positive attitude and the *flyness* of her wardrobe maintained by her mom. One day, a few months into our sisterhood, my little sister handed me her telephone and said, "My uncle wants to talk to you." Although he said we'd met once before, I didn't remember him. Even though the conversation was brief, I was interested. I knew his family so I felt like I knew him. While I should have been focused on my schooling, or perhaps being a mother to my 4 year-old son, or even on being a big sister and mentor to a very special young lady, I could only think of the possibility of him and me. He wanted me. None of those responsibilities, or the red flags that should have been flying around in my head, mattered to me as much as someone wanting me. Although I was all grown up, emotionally I was back in Benning Terrace trying to decide if I wanted "better" or if I wanted "now". After a couple of minutes of conversation, he asked me a question I wasn't expecting.

"Can I call you collect?"

Before his question could register in my brain, an automated female voice interrupted the call and informed us that there was only one-minute remaining.

"Huh?" I thought but had to play it off.

Clearly everyone knew what was going on except me. I had to make a decision and I had less than one minute to do it. Would I offend my little sister and her family and act as if I was too good for her uncle? Or would I throw caution to wind and ignore every red flag/emergency flare that was going off in my head?

I said, "Yes."

NEVERTHELESS

Turns out, he wasn't in jail for a minor offense. I'd heard the neighborhood gossip about him being a member of the gang led by a young man named Kevin Gray. What I didn't know was he wasn't just *in the gang*, he was supposedly an enforcer and helped to orchestrate murders on behalf of the gang. He was facing life in prison. The U.S. Attorney was prosecuting him and eight other defendants for crimes that ranged from drug dealing and racketeering to money laundering, witness tampering and murder. This was not going to be as simple as I had hoped. The trial gained a tremendous amount of public attention because the federal prosecutor decided to pursue the death penalty despite the fact that D.C. was not a death penalty jurisdiction. Because the nature of the gang's affairs functioned like a business, a business of committing murders to maintain the hold they had on drug sales in the city, the media began calling the case the Murder Inc. trial.

My little sister's uncle represented everything I wasn't supposed to be attracted to and yet I was. Attesting to the emotional highs that most women in love with an incarcerated man swear by, I can say that I loved the letters, phone calls (albeit collect and costly), and the expressiveness in his eyes during my weekly visits at the city jail. In reflection, I can see how the attraction I had for him was more about the void I had in me rather than the love either of us had, or supposedly had, for one another. Because he was incarcerated, I viewed him as someone who needed me more than any man had ever before. That need equated to love in my eyes but, in reality, it was a sign of a co-dependent sickness.

Though we talked every day, he was essentially unavailable and unable to love me the way I needed from a man. I was familiar with an unrewarding relationship and was addicted to loving someone who had no idea how to love me back. This was the summation of my life thus far. I was able to deny my own needs in order to focus on his. Being with him had all the ingredients of becoming the most sabotaging relationship I have ever been. Only, I was oblivious to the destructive presence it brought to my life. The love I had to give and needed to receive, was deliberately reduced to fit what he was able to provide me and receive from me. I deferred my need for love, physical and emotional attention, nurturing and security until a time when we would be together. I wasn't prepared to face my own fears or allow myself to believe that I deserved more than what I could get out of this relationship. I believed I would be rewarded one day, if only I got through this day. My new faith, I put in him rather than in God.

My family and friends were unable to understand how someone with *book sense* could be so naïve. I wanted to prove to the world that someone could love me, someone could want to take care of me, and that there was in fact someone who would never leave me - even if he couldn't leave his 6x8 cell.

Eventually, he chose to cooperate with the government in exchange for a new life in the Department of Justice Witness Security Program. On the streets, it's known as witness protection but it's the same program that protected criminals such as Mario "Sonni" Riccobene and Frank Lucas. His decision to go into the program meant I would never see or talk to him again, and never actually experience what I had spent the last few months telling everyone I already had. The only way to ensure I would get the love I had been telling people he gave me was enter into the program with him. It was a scary proposal. The premise of the program is to keep people safe from the people who want to see them killed. Sensing my hesitation, he asked me what I really wanted to hear. He asked if I would become his wife before we left and I said yes. I wouldn't be like my mom and turn down a proposal, even if it was just as unromantic and lacking sincerity as the one she received. Unbeknownst to me, what I thought was his desire to spend the rest of his life with me, was actually his contrived manipulation of protecting himself under spousal confidentiality from anything he possibly told me that could be used against him.

When I received the call that my enrollment in the program was approved, I prepared to leave everything behind. I surrendered my brand new car and all my belongings, and left for a life unknown. We became John, Jane and Baby Doe. Entering the witness security program meant giving up my birth name and birthplace, my entire personal, education and work history, which included the bachelor of architecture degree I had just earned. Contact with family and friends would be monitored closely by the U.S. Marshals. No one was to know where we were, where we were going, or from where we had come.

NEVERTHELESS

I didn't care. I had found love.

Literally, a person entering the program must board a plane with only the clothes on their back and one piece of luggage, which was thoroughly checked by the Marshals for anything prohibited. No identification. No money. No belongings. If the plane crashed, there would have been no public record that we were ever on it. My son and I were picked up in a black van with tinted windows and thick black curtains to prevent us from seeing out and any passersby from seeing in. We were driven to the Ronald Reagan Washington National Airport and from Washington, D.C. we flew first to Montgomery, Alabama and then a few days later, Little Rock, Arkansas. While in the program, I concentrated on starting our new lives with new identities. I knew his focus would be on his commitment to the case and his obligation to testify, so I tolerated behavior from him that I would not normally have if we were home. I wanted it to work. But I couldn't shake how familiar it all felt.

When running away from something or someone out of fear, there's a need to constantly be in a state of movement and capable of dropping everything if necessary. A willingness and openness to starting over and the ability to leave everything behind without looking back are important to someone who is on the run and hoping to never be found. My mom taught me well and was my perfect example of how to leave everything and everyone behind. Starting over was a something I was unapologetically proficient. My mom's decision to leave our home in Charlotte, in secret, for a new life was now being repeated in my life yet I didn't realize it.

The difference between my mom's decision to leave John and my decision to leave D.C. was that she left to flee an abusive relationship and I left to start one.

11

My first marriage lasted all of one year before I did the only thing I knew how to do. I left. It was no surprise that the witness security program would take some adjusting for both of us; he was being reintroduced back into society but not the society he was used to, and I now had to adjust to having nothing.

Our issues began as soon as we arrived in Little Rock. I am not sure how the Marshals decide which cities to move informants to, whether they even consider if we'd fit in or stand out, whether we will attract attention or make friends, but Little Rock was definitely a shock to our D.C. roots. I settled on the reality that they couldn't care less. Their job is to protect those who want to be protected, to help protectees get on their feet and become productive members of society. Honorable enough, but when you move a junior high dropout and drug dealer from Southeast D.C., possessing no professional skills to a middle-class non-minority neighborhood, it makes me wonder just how committed they are to ensuring protectees are able to integrate into their new identities and not return to their old ways.

That's exactly what happened with my first husband.

The pressure was great. We not only had to figure out our new lives in a new place, with new names, but we also had to learn how we fit together as a couple. When we left for the program, we had never spent longer than 30 minutes together, sitting across a visiting room table in a detention center. He began to feel trapped and resented leaving home. Added to his depression was the realization that he had committed to being a snitch against the men whom, at one point, he saw as family. He struggled with knowing he would eventually have to sit across from the same people that he ran the streets with, partied with, traveled with, laughed with, and loved. Now he was cooperating with the government to make sure they never saw freedom again. His anger and depression began to manifest in violence toward me. He started drinking, smoking weed and visiting the casinos in Memphis, TN. But it was when he became physically violent that I knew I had to leave.

Leaving him was a hard decision for me. I called the pastor of the church I had started attending, and after sharing my situation with him, he told me although he couldn't advise me to divorce him, that God never intended for me to be abused by my husband. I had to leave. I was embarrassed and ashamed. I didn't want to admit that he didn't love me. I tried to make excuses for him and even considered giving him another chance, but I couldn't risk my little boy. I had to leave for him. At that moment, I knew exactly how my mom felt in making the decision to leave. Staying meant remaining in an environment that held a level of familiarity despite the abuse while leaving brought the fear of uncertainty and change.

Victims of domestic violence come to a point of decision when they must weigh staying against leaving. Some stay and continue to live the horrors of abuse. Some leave and go on to be successful. Then there are those who pay the price of their life when they try to leave. People on the outside of the abuse easily assume leaving is just a simple decision but when the quality of life for your children will suffer, it is very difficult to leave. After a period of enduring the abuse, embarrassment and shame for staying become the chains that make leaving difficult. Until a victim can truly look at him or herself as too valuable to be treated that way, he or she will stay trapped in a torment of escalating abuse.

All the years I blamed and criticized my mom for leaving John, leaving our home and never looking back, I finally understood and saw her strength. Unfortunately, when women do muster up the courage to leave, strong is not how they see themselves and are often times treated as if they were the ones in the wrong for either getting into the relationship in the first place, or for not getting out earlier. Battered women have pressures against them from all sides.

NEVERTHELESS

I couldn't go home. I didn't want to admit that everyone who told me not to give up my life was right to be skeptical. I asked the agent assigned to our family if I could remain in the program, and although I was given permission, I was forced to pack up and move again because my marriage had ended. Two protectees familiar with one another from their past could not be located in the same area. They moved us both, me to Houston, TX and him to a place kept secret from me. This meant starting over yet again with a new name, new social security number, and a new false background story to memorize. With this, Sharonda Anderson was created.

For years, I was just one person who was trying to live a mediocre life, stay afloat and out of trouble. I had a son. I had given up most of my life for a man who turned out to be incapable of loving anyone or seeing past his own pain. I still had not figured out what was missing in my life, but I did know with all certainty that being with a man who made me feel worse about myself was not the missing piece. After living in Houston for one year, I decided I had to go home. I was slowing dying on the inside while alone in Houston. My anxiety was so much worse and often times I was unwilling to leave my apartment. Thankfully I met a young lady who helped me through this period and encouraged me to get the help I needed. I had to think about my son and the only family we had was back in D.C.

Broken, ashamed and empty, I moved back home full of resentment for all that I had given up. There I was a new person with no history. My old identity now belonged to the U.S. Marshals and my new identity lacked an education, work experience, credit or proof of birth. We were given passports in the program not birth certificates. Although the passport is considered the highest level of identification, simple tasks like registering a child for school requires a birth certificate to show the name of the parent. Each year and every time the school administrator contacted me, I lied and said I was working on getting a copied of everything they needed.

The truth was that I could never get a copy of the birth certificate for the boy whose identity was made up two years prior. I couldn't even explain why our last names differed or prove that I was his mother. This was the worst feeling yet. Even with all that I

NEVERTHELESS

had given up, not being able to prove that I was my son's mother was more than I could stand. I wanted to disappear. I wanted to stop making mistakes and was afraid that every decision I made and would make would be the wrong one. I didn't trust myself. I couldn't trust myself with my son. I hated what I had become and I was mad at God for allowing me to do this to myself. Yes, I said I was mad at God. I blamed God for the decisions I had made and for the consequences that had come from those decisions.

Wow! Have you ever been mad at God for something you thought was His fault for allowing? If you have, then we were both wrong! I wanted to do things my way. I relied only on myself, made my own decisions without once asking Him if this was what He wanted for me. And if I did pray, it wasn't for guidance so much as it was for a granted wish, as if God is a genie in a bottle. The speed bumps that God had placed in my life to slow me down, I completely bulldozed over them at full speed. Times when He sent an interceptor or someone to direct me another way, I ignored them. I wanted what I wanted and I convinced myself that a loving Father would give it to me. This is what the enemy wants. He wants to confuse us about what love is so we will fail to operate in the God-faith necessary to live the life that He has pre-destined. I had accepted Christ as Lord. I had joined a church. I had gotten married. This, I thought, was what I was supposed to do. Was I being punished? Why wasn't *my way* blessed?

Before I go any further, I want to address punishment, feeling forsaken or cursed for turning away from God. The enemy has one job to do, to separate us from the love of God, and he is very dedicated to this job. It's good for us that our Father is a forgiving and wonderful Father. He loves you and I so much that He gave of Himself for us. His Word became flesh so that we could have life and have it more abundantly. God didn't punish me nor did He forsake me.

> *"Be strong and of a good courage, fear not, nor be afraid of them: for the Lord thy God, he it is that doth go with thee; he will not fail thee, nor forsake thee."*
>
> Deuteronomy 31:6

NEVERTHELESS

Everyone will face burdens and situations that are either designed to bring us down (*crafted by the enemy*) or permitted to lift us up (*allowed by God*). Jesus never promised that our lives would be free from adversity, pain, or struggle. In fact, Jesus said specifically that we *WILL* have tribulation but in Him we *CAN* have peace. But what most see as God forsaking them is simply us testing our own faith. Yes, I said, us. The traps of the enemy do not establish our faith, but how we respond will determine if we believe what we say we believe, or if we're not really sure and just testing it out.

In Christ, we have been given the ability to walk by faith, a measure of faith and a source from which all our strength flows. Without testing what we have, or practicing what we believe, we miss the full understanding of our possession.

> *"Count it all joy, my brothers when you meet trials of various kinds, for you know that the testing of your faith produces steadfastness."*
>
> James 1:2-3

Secondly, every action has a consequence, either good or bad. Every situation is a lesson, either taught or learned. I couldn't expect to do what I wanted to do and not reap the fruit of it or face the consequences of my actions. I should have submitted all my fears unto God but I held them even closer. I didn't have revelation of Holy Spirit as my Comforter and my Guide. I didn't know the voice of God and therefore I was like a person unable to hear, walking in a dark forest and unable to see clearly. God's hand is always outstretched to us, beckoning and drawing us near to Him but when we hold our hands to our chest, afraid to extend them outward to catch His grasp, then we continue to stumble and fall. God was with me in my wilderness. He protected me from the things I could not bear and gave me a way of escape that I didn't always take right away. He extended His grace and His mercy toward me through it all and placed people in my life to help me when I needed it the most. I couldn't see His love and even when I acted like He wasn't in my life, He was.

For the next two years I lived a life that was less than God's desire for me or honestly, my desire for myself. I behaved foolishly. Although I vowed never again to attempt to take my own life, because I didn't want my son to feel like his love for me or my love for him was insufficient, I instead lived as if I didn't care if it came to an early end. I sent my son away to live with Grandma Toots who had by this time moved to North Carolina. She took him in without hesitation. Clearly, God's hand was at work in sending this family to me. Unfortunately, I didn't see it as an opportunity to draw closer to Him. I did just the opposite. I tried everything to distance myself from anything that reminded me of love, God's, mine or my son's. I began living recklessly day-to-day, with no care for tomorrow.

One night following a party, where I had been hired to perform as an exotic entertainer (*okay, a stripper*), I drove to my mom's house, drunk beyond belief. Proudly, I wanted to show her my stack of dollar bills. At 2 a.m., I knocked on her door, reeking of liquor and excitedly waved the bills in her face when she opened the door.

"Where on earth did you get that?"

"From stripping!" I barely got out coherently.

"Oh wow! Look at you! Get it girl! If your momma could do it, I would!"

"Yaaaazzzz!" I said, and with that I turned and stumbled my way down her front steps and back to my seat behind the wheel of my car.

"Bye baby. See you later," she said as she watched me navigate her stairs and get into my car.

"Bye ma!" I said and drove off.

That night, I failed to see the dangers in how I was living or in the decisions I made, particularly when I chose to drive drunk. My mom didn't seem concerned, my friends were doing the same thing, and my son was being raised by someone who loved him. The only regret I had came the following mornings in the form of a hangover from excessive drinking. As long as I took enough aspirin to get through the workday, then I could pretend my life was as I wanted. Eventually my drunk driving would have legally punishable consequences and it would be those consequences that forced me to see myself for who I was becoming and how I was living.

NEVERTHELESS

On a different night, after taking in several vodka drinks with a guy at a local D.C. bar, I decided to make my way to my home in Maryland. At first the journey was fine but then it quickly began to play out like a scene on television. The windows were rolled down and the sunroof of my Scion was open to the stars in the night sky above. I was blasting the tunes of Beres Hammond and my mind drifted back and forth from the road ahead of me to the island sands of Tortola. The brisk chill of the night, the perfect music, the clear road ahead free of traffic. I would get home in no time. That was until something caught my eye on my left. It was another car.

Seems someone wanted to race.

80mph. 90mph. Lane switching, cat and mouse as we sped up the Baltimore-Washington Parkway. Adrenaline flowed through my veins and amplified my already intoxicated and induced state. But then the other car slowed drastically, almost coming to a stop. In my rearview mirror, the other car grew smaller and smaller as my distance in front grew larger and larger. I was winning!!! No, correction, I WON!!! Then I saw the red and blue lights flashing behind me. *Should I stop?* I wondered. Then I answered myself, *nope.*

Instantly, as if on cue, Beres stopped singing and in my head the voices of Inner Circle started with "Bad Boys" as loud as the music from the speakers. I was in my own episode of the television show *Cops* and, unlike all the stupid criminals who always seemed to get caught on every episode, I was going to get away.

One car with flashing lights, then two police cars with flashing lights to finally three cars and a helicopter. I decided I should pull over. I turned on my turn signal and took the next exit, which happened to be the turn off for the Prince George's Hospital. With guns drawn, the officers approached my car. With my hands on the wheel, I yelled through the window opening, "What seems to be the problem officer?"

"Get out of the car now!!!"

I got out and the officer realized I was more of a wreck to myself than a threat to him. He asked me why didn't I pull over when he first pulled behind me and I answered that I wasn't sure he was police officer. There had been stories of women getting pulled over by someone they thought was an officer because of flashing lights, only to be raped on the side of the road. He wasn't impressed with my story. I was required to take a sobriety test, which I failed, and told shortly after to put my hands behind my back.

The cuffs went on and the officer placed me in the back of his cruiser. Still in character in my imaginary episode titled, "Caught by the tireless pursuit of Maryland Park Police", I started looking for the dashboard camera. Forgetting the camera is usually facing outward to catch all that happens in front of the vehicle, I was trying to position myself to get my best side on screen. I could still hear a helicopter overhead, which I determined was part of my chase and had absolutely nothing to do with the emergency room of the hospital just around the corner. As I continued to move around trying to get in a good position, the officer yanked open the door and yelled at me to be still. "The more you move, the tighter the seatbelt is going to get so unless you want to choke yourself, YOU BETTER BE STILL!"

Why is it that alcohol intoxication causes extreme hysterics then an emotional outpouring of tears? No other part of the evening upset me like when he yelled at me. It was as if my dad, whom I wouldn't know if he was standing in front of me, or for all I knew could have very well been that officer, was yelling at me out of disappointment and shame. By the time, we reached the Greenbelt holding station, I was on my way down from my euphoric state. Once the inebriation subdued, and I realized it was real life and not an episode of *Cops*, I entered into a state of pitiful regret.

At this point, the officer ran my prints and entered my social. But something was wrong. He said it must be a computer glitch. He asked me where was I from and immediately I knew it was because my social security number was only two years old. It was like throwing ice water into my face and I immediately sobered up. It was too late, of course, to avoid the charges but I was aware enough to remember to say I was from Oklahoma, not Charlotte, N.C. so my birthplace matched my new social security number.

He went on to tell me how blessed I was that the night didn't end in my death or the death of another person.

NEVERTHELESS

I told him I was a mother and that made me feel worse. I told him I was a college graduate, never in trouble before, and that made me feel stupid. I told him I was sorry and that made me feel grateful that I still had life and breath to say those words. Then it hit me, how was I to get home?

No one can ever say my God doesn't provide a way. Even when we cut up like pure fools, He is there. Even when we are undeserving, He is there. And even when I decided to drink and drive, He was there to cover me and those around me that night with the protection that only a wonderfully forgiving Father can provide.

I told the officer that I didn't have anyone to call and that I was all alone. I asked if I could walk home and he said no. By the time my processing was complete, it was 4 a.m. and I knew the chances of waking anyone up to come get me would be slim to none. The officer told me I either had to find someone to pick me up or prepare to sleep on the concrete bench/bed in the cell. I shrugged and got ready to take my place on the bench then a second officer came in and said, "Your ride is here."

"What ride? No one but you, me and God knows I'm here." I said.

"He says he's here to pick you up and knows your name."

I got up and went to the front of the station. At the door stood the guy who I had been out drinking with earlier. He said he called my phone to check on me to make sure I had gotten home okay and a man answered. The man was the tow truck driver who retrieved my car after my arrest. The tow truck driver told the guy I had been taken in by the Park Police and gave him the address of the station. He then came immediately to get me out. The tears returned and I walked out, in his arms, still carrying my shoes in my hands.

As I write this, I can barely hold back the tears. Not just because of how I allowed myself to become so out of control, but because of how grateful I am for all that didn't happen. Sometimes our focus is on all that is lacking or on the things we wish had occurred, rather than centering in on the blessings we receive when God prevents the things that would destroy us. Even when I was in my most pitiful state, God's

NEVERTHELESS

mercy and love far exceeded and extended beyond anything I could comprehend. That night my son could have lost his mother. That night an innocent person could have lost their life. I am deeply grateful neither came to be.

Even when our mountains are self-created, God still makes a way out of what seems like there's no way of escape. As punishment, I was sentenced to 18 months of probation and required to attend Alcoholics Anonymous meetings, as well as a meeting of MADD (Mothers Against Drunk Driving) to see firsthand the consequences that can come from driving under the influence. I spoke with others in my group classes and it amazed me how, even in my filth and disobedience, God protected me from the worse it could have been. While others were getting suspended licenses and thousand-dollar fines, I received probation and an $80 fine. While others who were arrested by county police received higher penalties and a state record, I was arrested by Maryland-National Capital Park Police, received a sealed record and my punishment was handled differently. A wrong turn, a tremendous err in judgement and yet God still saw fit to protect me and those around me. While recognizing that my actions were grossly reckless, I refuse to allow shame to rob me of the opportunity to give God the praise for keeping me in spite of myself. I know my story is not unique.

Have you ever expected to receive consequences for your actions only to have them waived or forgiven? Have you ever expected to have to pay a ticket, fee or infraction only find out it was canceled? Or perhaps you were culpable for something more serious like my misjudgment, and after repenting, you're prepared to receive judgment only to find out your obligation has been paid in full? In the moment of forgiveness, we have a choice of how to respond. Either we can allow guilt and shame to convince us we were and will always be undeserving of God's grace, or we can choose to be forever and humbly grateful, walk in repentance and acceptance of God's love and forgiveness. The enemy would rather have us look at those moments in our lives when we failed or when things didn't seem to go quite right and be sadden by or ashamed of them. Then every day that follows will be overshadowed with justifying why we didn't deserve God's love in the first place. Remember this is what the goal of the devil, to separate us from the love of God.

Or perhaps the guilt you feel is because you don't understand why you were kept away from the consequences or results that others may have had to endure for the same act of sin. God's protection is not something to be ashamed of or feel guilty for having access to. I know there are believers who made the same decisions I've made but have had different, or even worse, outcomes. But I understand that my life is not more or less worthy than anyone else's. I would never attempt to explain why things happen the way they do. I trust in God's plan for every believer's life and recognize that only the enemy gains reward in our comparison with one another. My job is to put my rest in God, knowing that His love is capable of healing all wounds and restoring hope. He is a just God who will repay you with a double portion of honor. He will give us beauty for ashes and an everlasting joy when we turn to Him in the midst of all tribulation. God looks at our hearts and our hearts must be turned to Him.

When God anointed David, it was the heart of David where God saw the position of king in him.

David was chosen because he was a man after God's own heart. It was David's heart to please God and therefore God orchestrated circumstances in David's life to protect him from persecutions and other attacks. What would have produced one consequence for someone else didn't produce the same consequences for David, simply because he lived a life that was at peace with God. (Psalm 4:8).

I know the seeds of love that I planted in the lives of others helped to position me for the protection I received. I know all the times before that night on Washington-Baltimore Parkway when I served others, forgave instead of finding fault, went to God on bended knee giving Him honor and worshipping His Name, helped to manifest the protection that I experienced on that night and the months to follow. God is our protector, shield and strength. Even through loss and bad decisions, we have to choose to see the blessings, grace and mercy that have been extended to us. Blessings are all around us, and we are actively a part of them. We are constantly in the position of both receiving and giving. God is just that awesome to create us to serve in two positions at once. The choice is yours which one you focus on.

NEVERTHELESS

We are blessed to be a blessing and we are forgiven to forgive. And it all begins with the person in the mirror. Receiving love from God is not always what people struggle with. It's accepting that God forgives us when we haven't figured out how to forgive ourselves. The key is to pick yourself up from what the enemy wants you to think is defeat and say to that situation *"still I rise!"* The Bible says that no weapon formed shall prosper but by omission it teaches us that weapons will in fact be formed. God's Word then assures us that we still have the victory. The power is still in you to overcome the pain of wrong choices. God's love is greater, bigger, better, and more than enough. He can take a dire situation and make it into one where you come out better than you were before. You just have to believe.

SHARONDA JONES

Enjoying the scenery of Frank Lloyd Wright's
Kentuck Knob in Chalk Hill, PA

12

Ideally, I would love to say after my brief late night run from the law and DUI conviction that I immediately turned my life around, went back to church, joined the choir, got back in God's Word and went on to do great work for the Kingdom of God. Eventually this would all happen, well, not the choir part because I don't think my singing would bring joy to anyone. My turnaround just didn't occur right away.

Despite how much anger and sadness I carried, regardless of how bitter I was about the path my life had taken, in my heart, love remained. It didn't matter how much I tried to suppress it, my desire for love remained. No matter how much I tried to run from God, His love remained and He continued to provide covering for me. I still desired a family. I continued to long for unconditional love, acceptance and security from another although I tried to convince myself that no one, not even God or myself could be trusted to fulfill my hearts desires.

When I met the man I would have my second child with, I was far from ready for a relationship. I was deep in my sinfulness and spent every second trying to convince myself that's where I belonged. I was 29 years old, living alone and without a single care. My son was living in North Carolina with Grandma Toots, and I still had not come to a definitive decision about what kind of life I wanted to live. Up to the day I learned of my pregnancy, I still had not been able to see past my pain to how God was continuing to bless me. I only saw that I was free to do as I pleased with whomever and wherever I pleased to do it. And that's what I did, up until the day I received a phone call from a nurse in the office of my Ob/Gyn.

NEVERTHELESS

"Ms. Anderson, we have your test results back and congratulations, you're pregnant."

"Huh? Are you serious?"

"Yes. Now, we need to schedule the first of your prenatal visits so we can make sure you have a healthy baby, ok? How's next week for you?"

"Ummm, okay I guess. Let me check my calendar and get back to you."

"Okay, but we need to get you in as soon as possible. Will the father be joining you at your visits? It would help to have him there so we can get answers from you both. Will that work?"

"Ummm...I'll ask and let you know."

"Okay dear. Don't delay. Goodbye."

"Goodbye."

Getting pregnant was the last thing I wanted. I had been seeing the same guy for over a year and he was pushing me for a more serious commitment. He wanted to marry me but I kept telling him I wasn't ready. I didn't know how to break the news to him that technically I was still married. But not just married, but married to a man whom I couldn't say for sure existed and by what name he did exist. Nor did I know how to break the news to him that technically I wasn't who I told him I was, and that I had only been this identity for the last four years.

How do I share in a conversation that my husband was a government witness in the largest racketeering, criminal enterprises, and murder case in D.C. since the Rayful Edmonds trial in the late 1980s? Do I mention it over breakfast, lunch or dinner that he helped to run a crack cocaine and heroin trade organization, and killed government witnesses to keep the business going? Do I share that I left him and he could very well be looking for me?

I decided to say nothing.

Since my participation in the program ended abruptly without any direction from the U.S. Marshals as to exactly how I was supposed to return to a normal life as a private citizen, I was unsure how to explain my situation to anyone, partly out of embarrassment and partly out of fear that the person knew about the case. For that reason, I limited what

NEVERTHELESS

I said and to whom I said anything about the case or the program.

Secondly, I didn't exactly know who I was legally. When we first entered the program, my name was Sharonda Andrews. But now that name was the property of the U.S. Marshals and the Department of Justice. It could never again be used by me. On paper and to every credit institution, I looked as if I just magically appeared out of thin air. Every day, I rehearsed and tweaked my backstory so that it would sound convincing. "Hi, my name is Sharonda Anderson and I was born in Oklahoma. I moved here two years ago, and no, I am not a terrorist." My goal was to avoid being reported to the Office of Homeland Security for a suspicious background.

The third reason for my hesitation (remember, most everything for me happens in 3s) was that I didn't know if I was still married or not. I married my husband before we entered the program. When our relationship ended and we separated, we were issued a second set of new identities and shipped off to two different states. I suppose then we weren't legally married anymore because technically the people we used to be no longer existed. But then I left the program, with a new name and story. Although I was home, I was not the same person. I was still Sharonda to family and friends but I wasn't the same person on paper or emotionally. I was confused about who I should be. I had to decide whether to return to my old ways or take the opportunity to start over as if I had amnesia. I chose a little of both.

Once I accepted the pregnancy, I decided maybe it would be good for us, a way to start my life over. I started looking forward to sharing the news with him. I waited until the night of the holiday party for his job. I bought him a Harley-Davidson brand picture frame that said 'Dad' and gave it to him when he picked me up for the party. When he opened it, the look of shock and excitement filled his face. We traveled the entire way talking about possible names and due dates, we were deep into planning our new life together by the time we reached the party. When we arrived, he introduced me to everyone he worked with including his boss. He told his boss our good news and we enjoyed the night talking and dreaming of our life with our new baby. He hoped for a boy and I wanted a girl.

NEVERTHELESS

A week later, I called him and told him we needed to talk. I told him everything and I could hear a change in his voice almost instantly. He told me he had to think about it and that he would let me know where things stood. I took what he said as just an initial reaction, I mean, the love I believed he had for me couldn't be over that fast or easy, right? I was carrying his baby. I was having this baby for him, for us, for our future. He wasn't going to leave me. He loved me. He would get over it. We would get through it. We were going to be a family.

He eventually called me days later, after ignoring my countless calls, text messages, and notes left on the front door of his house. What he said I will never forget because it felt as if it destroyed my world.

"You need to have an abortion."

"What did you say?"

"I thought about it and I decided I don't want a baby. Not with you."

"No. You can't. You can't do this. Just take more time. Just think a little longer. How can you say this to me?"

He hung up.

I felt like I hadn't explained it right, and that there was something, one thing that I could say to make it all better and make him remember he still loved me. If only he would take my calls. If only he would hear me out. But he wouldn't. I found out later what he really wanted was someone to help him out financially. By marrying him, he would be in a better tax situation and with a dependent to claim, he could finally get out of the tax burden he was under and no longer be a risk of losing his home. He didn't want me. He wanted the benefit of what I could bring to his finances. The fact that I couldn't marry him because of my identity issues was a deal breaker for him.

But that wasn't the worst of it.

He, too, had secrets. He wasn't being completely honest about a little thing called monogamy. He was adamant about the abortion because, since I couldn't marry him, he decided he would marry his side chick. This meant he didn't want her to find out about the baby we were having. Finding out that he didn't love me was hard, learning he had another woman on the side was even harder, but the fact that he wanted me to end the life growing inside me to keep his secret made me feel dead inside. The only thing that continued to give me life, was the life growing inside me.

There I was yet AGAIN... lied to, abandoned, and confused. I knew how much he wanted a child and I was ready to settle down like he had been asking me to do from the beginning of our relationship. At a few months shy of my 30th birthday, my life had gone full circle to end up back at scratch. My son was still living in N.C. and wasn't required to witness firsthand the mess of a life. I was now just like my mom, I had sent my child away with no idea of how or when I would be able to get him back.

I considered the abortion he wanted me to have. I felt like I was nothing and I had nothing to offer. I was carrying my second child, by a man who wanted nothing to do with me or the baby, and I had no idea where I would go from there. All I could manage to do was go to work and back home, and then repeat on autopilot. I tried to turn off my emotions. Though I had started going back to church, when I found out I was pregnant, I stopped again. The idea of going back to church as a single mother who was now pregnant with another child out of wedlock filled me with more shame than I had before. Church was the last place I wanted to be, and the enemy was pleased with that decision.

What I didn't understand at that time was although I didn't want to go to church, as a child of God through acceptance of Jesus Christ, I am the Church. I may not have needed the physical structure of brick and mortar, I did need the Word of God to sustain and restore me. We should not allow Satan to keep us away from fellowship with our brothers and sisters in Christ. We need that interaction, exchange and, sharpening of iron in the battles of spiritual warfare. I was ignorant to any of this. I was still trying to live "of this world" in this world. I told myself I had to have the abortion, which I knew meant taking a life; regardless of the connection I had already begun to develop with the baby growing inside me. Carrying and delivering him or her would take more out of me than I thought I had in me to give. I wasn't even sure I wanted this baby for myself. I told myself I was having this baby for him. I didn't need another child. I needed a drink.

NEVERTHELESS

Besides, he was right. I couldn't do this by myself. I couldn't do this to him. I couldn't do this to this baby. Just when I began to believe I had no one who could fully understand the pain I was in, I remembered there's one person in this entire world who has felt a pain greater than one I could ever imagine and yet she survived. She, despite her faults and flaws, raised me the best she could and didn't abort me or give me up no matter how desolate or downtrodden she was. The last person I thought I could turn to was in fact the only person I could turn. My mom. The same person who watched me make poor decisions and supported them. The same person who had made her own share of poor decisions and, now not even sure about her own spirituality, was the person God used.

I told her I wanted to have an abortion. I asked her to pray for me and to tell me what to do.

I was in total shock by her response. I had fully expected my mom to revert to her new age beliefs or ancestral worship and prayers, medicinal herbs, and spiritual bath concoctions, or even suggest that I participate in an animal sacrifice ritual to help ease my pain, unblock my orisha blessings or perhaps to put a voodoo hex on my baby's daddy. But she did none of this. She simply held me in her arms as I cried and said, "Remember your faith."

"Huh?"

"I want you to remember your faith," she repeated. "Remember all that your pastor has taught you and what the Bible says. You belong to God and He is your Father. He will protect you and take care of you. So please, baby, please don't kill my grandchild. I love him or her."

I looked up to find her eyes, partly because I wanted to make sure she hadn't been replaced by a mock version of herself. It was her and I was certain she meant everything she said. In fact, let me change that, it wasn't her saying it to me, it was Holy Spirit speaking to me through her. Of course it was her face, the lips of her mouth moving and the sound of her voice as she spoke, but the message she uttered spoke directly to my spirit as only Holy Spirit can do.

I can't say that the skies opened up or that angels descended from heaven like movies often portray, but what happened in that room on that day, at that moment was something no movie director could capture or imitate. I was reminded of something greater and more substantial than what I was going through. My mom held me as I continued to cry. I thanked her between sobs for being there and for helping me through. I remembered feeling like she handled this situation far better than when I was 14 but then shouldn't growth be for everyone? God had given me yet another gift. And God used my mom to deliver it. He used the most unexpected person to reach me and touch me at my core.

Following that experience, everything changed, though it may have taken months even years for the fullness to manifest. I moved into my own apartment, a 1-bedroom 2nd-floor unit over a hair salon, and then went to N.C. to bring my son home. In August 2006, I gave birth to a healthy and beautiful 5-pound baby girl and the three of us started the newest chapter of our family journey.

I didn't know what the future would hold but I had hope and, for the first time in a very long time, having hope didn't terrify me. It may have seemed as if I was setting myself up to repeat the same cycles that I had gone through with my son but it didn't feel that way to me. I couldn't put my finger on it at the time but I believed I would be okay. I had a second chance at motherhood and I had to do it right this time. I couldn't take the responsibility of motherhood and life the same way I had taken when it was just my son and me. On the surface, it appeared I was just a single mother who was already struggling with one kid who was inevitably going to struggle more with two kids. But there was more to me this time.

I decided I wouldn't allow the enemy to have any more of my joy. I would raise my kids up in the Word and they would know the Lord from an early age. I started attending church regularly again and had my little baby girl dedicated to God on February 4, 2007. With my family and friends, I stood at the altar as my pastor blessed my precious baby girl. As it was obvious there was no man standing next to me where the father would have stood, my Man of God saw into my spirit and answered the question I had never spoken aloud. He said my child has a Father who will never leave her nor forsake her. She was covered and would be taken care of. She was loved and I knew we would all be fine.

I simply had to give God what He wanted; I had to give God my heart.

NEVERTHELESS

Dear God,

I surrender my all to you. I only have room for what you want to put in my life, in my heart, in my spirit. Father, I thank you for loving me beyond what I could have ever imagined was possible. I repent for not trusting in You, for not having an ear to hear from You, and for thinking that I can do this life without You. Thank for allowing me a second chance. Thank you for giving me saving Grace through your Son, Jesus. Thank you for comforting me and keeping me so that I may come to know the peace that only You can give. I decrease so that You may increase in my life. I submit to You Lord God so that I may come to see the life of victory that you have for me. Thank you for the thoughts that you have toward me, thoughts of peace and not of evil, to give me a future and a hope.

In Jesus name, Amen.

With that, I stopped looking for love and decided to only focus on being a mom to my kids. The following year, in 2007, despite having a social security number with flags, limited credit and little employment history in my new name, I purchased my first home and was establishing a foundation for myself and my kids. The following year, my First Lady, Dr. Dee Dee Freeman held her God's Glamourous Girls Conference at the convention center where I worked. The director of audio visual services worked the event directly. On the last night of the event, I emailed him to ask why the screens in the ballroom bounced as much as they did. It was a distraction and I thought he should be aware. I was an administrative assistant and he was the head of audio visual services department, so I never imagined he would even take the time to respond. But he did. I know for a fact God put our meeting in motion because there's no other way to explain it.

By that September, we were dating. By the following February, we were married.

Yes, prayer surely changes things, without a doubt.

NEVERTHELESS

RISE

"What lies behind us, and what lies before us are but tiny matters compared to what lies within us."

—RALPH WALDO EMERSON

13

Faith. Faith. Faith. Say it three times and it will appear. Well, no not really. Faith comes by hearing and hearing by the Word of God. Hebrews 11:1 states that "faith is the substance of things hoped for, the evidence of the things not seen." Every aspect about being a Christian radiates from a central core of faith. Without faith, we have nothing. The enemy knows that if he can rob us of our confidence and hope, then we are bound by an inability to walk by faith.

Having hope meant looking forward to the realization of things I wanted. No one hopes for bad things to happen to them, right? But for most of my young life, whenever I allowed myself to be hopeful or look forward to something good, I expected bad things to follow. Consequently, I limited what I wanted or desired to the level of my situation, and when I truly put effort in it, I was able to reduce my hope to almost nonexistent. That was one of my coping mechanisms. As I got older, and had more control over my life and how I lived it, I allowed myself to hope for only what I could devise a plan and subsequent backup plan to get. If I couldn't figure it out, then I didn't expect it to come to pass. My faith was only as far as my hands could reach, my eyes could see or by my means accomplish.

Eventually, as I matured in the Word of God, I learned to accept that nothing in my life happens by accident but rather is an orchestrated, cause and effect, consequential byproduct of a prior act or predestined plan for my life. Even with predestined plans, I had to be a willing participant. From the only one of my mom's three children to survive and raised by her without any contact or help from my father, my life story did not develop as anyone would dream or idealize.

As some saw the growth in me that seemed to exceed them in life, they tried to delay my progress by shaming me for outgrowing them. "Don't forget where you came from", they would say, as if I could ever forget. If I could, I would do everything in my power to do just that – **forget** my past, them and everything I endured! But I have not forgotten and I know why. I remember so I can use my story just as I'm doing now, to help others who may be going through the same struggles of abandonment, depression, shame, guilt or feelings of worthlessness. And yet I still find it interesting how the phrase "don't forget where you came from" can create a false sense of bondage for so many people.

"Soar eagle, on wings outstretched and strong enough to carry you far...but only as far as this chain attached to your leg will allow you to go," used to be my thought when someone told me not to forget where I came from. Usually delivered by individuals' whose lives have not improved as much as the person to whom this statement is being directed, it is intended to cause them to surrender, cease or slow in their drive or forward movement toward a better life for themselves.

Growing up, I would often hear the statement, "like crabs in a barrel" which simply means if all couldn't escape, then no one would. That's how it was when I began to turn my life around and made the decision to pursue a Godly lifestyle. It was as if I had to pay retribution for trying to experience freedom from the barrel. The people I used to go out drinking and partying with were the least receptive of my newfound pursuit of a Proverbs 31 type of virtue. Behind me were the days of debauchery but some of my former friends received my growth with contempt, believing my new posture of righteousness would be used to belittle them for the lifestyle that they continued to live.

My old ways shouldn't continue once I learned how to be and do better. Those who have not experienced the same growth in maturity, wisdom or understanding may not agree with the change that comes as a result of revelation and that's okay. It is okay to say, "No, I don't do that anymore" or "I stopped doing it that way." The goal is to avoid directing judgment or condemnation toward those who have yet to reach that place; instead, we are to continue to walk in the love of Jesus just as we wanted them to do with us prior to our awakening.

NEVERTHELESS

Deliberately deciding to make positive changes in your life, enriching the lives of those around you, and living a life that honors Christ is not "forgetting where you come from" but rather acknowledging where you're going. It is understanding fully and remembering from where one has been delivered and accepting the change necessary to have a better life and a richer experience while here on earth. It is understanding that with God, a woman like Rahab who lived during the time of the Prophet Joshua with a nefarious reputation, can become part of the genealogy for the Coming of Jesus Christ. Making the choice to leave a shameful life for one that is guiltless and restored is not forgetting where you came from, it is having faith for a future of grace, favor, and restoration that God has already planned for you.

Twenty years after my mom packed our bags in the middle of the night and whisked me away from our home in Charlotte, I returned as an adult to visit the house where I had such fond memories. It appeared to be half the size as I remembered it. I knocked on the door and explained to the person who answered that I used to lived there as a little girl and asked if I could come in. Now looking back, I'm not sure if the more shocking part is that I asked to enter a stranger's house or that the stranger allowed me to enter based on the story of "I used to live here." Either way, I wasn't prepared for what I saw. The passageway between the living room and dining room was closed off. What I remembered as the dining room was now a bedroom and the kitchen didn't seem large enough for one person to work in, least alone two. Rooms that I remembered as light and airy were in this reality cramped and overcrowded. My old room belonged to a little boy as indicated by the blue walls and toy trucks strewn across the floor. Immediately, I began to feel overwhelmed with emotion; I thanked the new resident for allowing me to walk through their home one last time and I left.

Recalling where I came from doesn't require me to stay there nor does it require me to feel any guilt or remorse for growing beyond. I no longer fit where I used to be and it was okay to acknowledge it. I simply did not fit, physically, emotionally, or mentally. I had grown up from the little girl that used to play in the yard of that home. I had grown up from the little girl who was full of fear and trust issues that stemmed from being abruptly uprooted from

NEVERTHELESS

what I thought was my foundation and my source of peace. I had grown up. I was beginning to rise.

Before leaving Charlotte, I drove to the area where I remembered playing with friends. Instead of an area large and open, filled with sounds of laughter, hope and freedom, I found a low-income housing development that had now fallen into a desolate state. It no longer had green grassy areas, playground equipment or friendly residents outside to welcome me. No one sat on their porch with a welcoming smile or with expressions of warmth like an extension of my family. Instead, I received skeptical stares and weary glances as my car slowly approached. I wanted to leave to protect the beautiful memories I had. I did not want my memories tarnished or destroyed by the reality of how it looked 20 years later. Charlotte 1977-79 was the memory I wanted to hold on to. I didn't have to forget, I just had to understand that I could never go back. The basis of our strength does not require going back to the pains of our past or even remembering what used to be. Our foundation is based on the One who brought us through them.

Reflecting does however help to reveal the strength given to us by God. This is why God allows us to retain our memories. He wants us to see all that He has kept us through and if we look close enough, we'll see some of what He has kept us from. Strength does not come from trial and tribulation. It is a gross misunderstanding to believe God gives us trials and tribulations to make us strong. Neither does our strength come from the attacks from the enemy or the warfare that we engage in spiritually. Our strength comes from a source much greater than my past pains or present trials. God is our refuge and strength. - *Psalm 46:1* When we turn to Him, and put our hope in the Lord, our strength is renewed. - *Isaiah 4:31* God gives us strength and He renews the strength that He gives. Struggle does not provide strength. It only pulls out what is already there.

By creation, women are strong. I have come to the realization that God created woman from man as to ensure her submission to his position in the relationship and creation. Not to say that men aren't strong in their own right as head of the house and all that jazz, but for women to have the responsibility of bearing and nurturing children, holding up her man, keeping her home, and look good doing it, proves that

NEVERTHELESS

we are an equally strong half of a whole creation made in the likeness of God.

God planned this when He created woman and in understanding the power that is placed inside her to be able to accomplish all she has to, He had to make sure it didn't go to her head by making her the head. Satan knew that by deceiving the woman, he could destroy the family. He also knew that by intriguing the woman, he could reach the man because of the woman's influence over man. Our curves, our intellect, our nurturing and our protection is life to our men, and equally we need them in return to love us as Christ loves the Church, to care for and protect us understanding that by doing this they are caring for and protecting every seed after them.

As women, we must remember our strength and our ability to separate pain from power. In my mom's own unique way, this is what she attempted to do for me after the sexual assault. She wanted me to separate myself from the pain of the abuse in order to overcome it. This was her way of coping with the abuse from her past but just as it didn't work for her, it didn't work for me. Only the Word of God was able to heal me from the pain of the abuse.

First, I had to forgive myself and then, as strange as it sounds, forgive my attacker for his actions. He took from me something that wasn't his to take. But he didn't take away the promises of God for my life. His actions didn't destroy me so instead of dealing with the pain, the Word of God says I am able to overcome it. Love covers a multitude of sin, ranging from the hate I felt toward him, toward myself, to the disappointment I felt toward my mom for not protecting me. Holding on to the pain was not moving me forward, rather it was holding me back. I had to see how strong I still am, how strong I was before the attack, during the attack and every day following. I had to see that the attack against me didn't change God's love for me nor did it denounce or disqualify me from the blessings already meant for me.

There's no taking away of responsibility and accountability from the young man who assaulted me because he committed a crime, a crime not only in statute but also in morality. Regardless of whether I was a virgin or a promiscuous teenager, regardless of

NEVERTHELESS

whether I fought him to his death or mine, regardless of whether we pressed charges or allowed shame to convict me of a crime I didn't commit. The enemy wanted that experience to destroy me, but it didn't. The enemy wanted that experience to shame me into silence and remorse but I refuse to be silent. I refuse to allow that moment to negatively frame or diminish the confidence I have in myself or steal my purpose from me. What the enemy envisioned would be my destruction, I choose to use to give honor to God. I choose to base my response to that which was done against me on the Word of God, the love of God, and the assurance in God to bring me out better than before. I choose to accept that what happened in the past does not determine my future, it only provides me with a choice of how to approach it.

Will I be angry, hurt or disappointed that my life lacked the presumed ease of others' lives, constantly comparing myself to them?

Will I hold onto offense because I felt acts against me were unwarranted or unfair?

Will I demand others to be accepting of me because of my past hurt, as if pain excuses my poor behavior or mean disposition?

Or will I be loving, accepting, humble, patient, and honorable as Jesus was to all, knowing that His life was not His own but rather given to the world so that we all might be saved?

While I understand saying we should approach every wrong ever done to us as Jesus did seems like a tall order for us, I have faith that God would not give us a role that would be impossible to fill. In Matthew 19:26, Jesus Himself told the disciples "with God all things are possible". We simply have to choose to take life one day at a time, rejoice in the fact that this is the day that the Lord has made for you and I to be victorious, and to have a life of abundant grace, favor and mercy.

You may have had an ideal and perfect life. You may have chosen to suffer in silence because of shame and guilt. You may have been convinced you allowed an offense because you did not fight the fight others thought you should have fought. You may have taken abuse from a husband or boyfriend, or are struggling

NEVERTHELESS

to carry the weight of scars from other kinds of battles. Either way, let me remind you that you are still worth the ransom paid on the Cross. You still have access and the right to proclaim victory through Christ. Even when it feels as though something was stripped away from you, let me remind you that you are still the whole, complete and treasure of God.

What's comforting about God's Word is that it is never changing, forever true and will always be a rock to stand on. There are no shells to shake, candles to burn, stars to be aligned, or other religious rituals and traditions to bring the Word of God to pass. The promises He has given us are simply "yes and Amen". The love He has is eternal and His grace is sufficient. When we are weak, He is our strength. When we are lost, He is our guide. When we are uncertain, He gives us wisdom. Shame, guilt, condemnation are all cares that Jesus took upon Himself for the world, and salvation by God's grace is a gift of the covenant confirmed by and in Christ Jesus.

Take a moment to look over your life to determine if there's anything that has held you captive; an unforgiveness, a hurt or disappointment that you have not been able to let go of. Allow Holy Spirit to comfort you and guide you through the release of any hold that unforgiveness has had on you up to this point. Allow yourself to be free from offense, against others and yourself. It is wonderful to hold on to hope. It is wonderful to love again. Just be sure to base both on your faith in God to keep you, nevertheless.

Prayer Pause

Father, in Jesus Name, I thank you for this opportunity to reflect on your love for me. Thank you for allowing me to grow in faith for the things that you have already provided for me and to cast away those things that are not given to me by you, like doubt, unforgiveness, fear and shame.

Lord God, I lean to you and to the strength that only You can give. I trust that with every trial there is a way of escape. I ask, Lord God, for you to reveal to me how I am to use my 'used to', my through, and my witness to glorify and honor you. My life is yours Lord and I submit to you so that I may grow and fulfill the purpose you have for me. Thank you, Father for your love, for your Word, and for the protection you have always provided over me. I choose to walk in love. I choose to walk in forgiveness. I choose you, Lord, so therefore I know I have the victory through Christ Jesus. Amen.

SHARONDA JONES

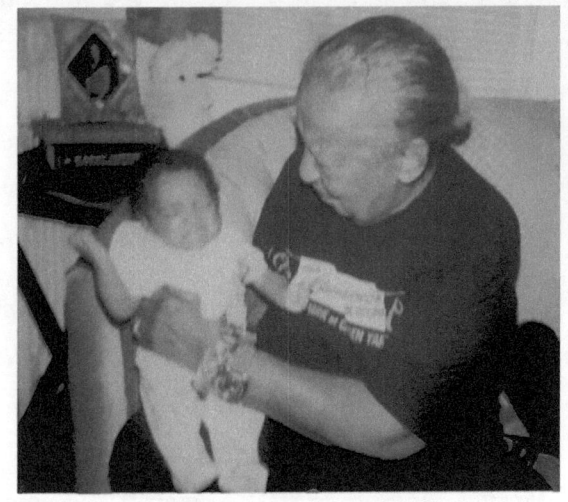

Grandma Toots and Maya

14

On July 15, 2016, a judge signed an order declaring my husband as the father to my middle child, a role he had been fulfilling for seven years prior to our day in court. We celebrated the event as if we had just given birth to a new baby. Our daughter didn't seem at all phased by the entire process though every adult was visibly and emotionally spent. When asked the days leading up to the hearing and on the day of how she felt, she replied simply, "My daddy was already my daddy." To her, we were only going to court to ask the judge for permission to change her name from

Anderson to Jones, which was in essence all we were doing, really.

No one, including my husband, seemed to be as affected as I was by it all. To him, just as to her, this was more a formality than a real life changing situation. He was already financially, emotionally, physically, mentally, and spiritually connected to and responsible for her. He would love her no more or no less regardless of what the court said. For him, this was just a legal requirement so he could never again have to hear "Sir, I will need to speak to her *real* parent," from a doctor, a teacher, or other official-type person. It bothered him deeply, and rightfully so, when taking her to the doctor for an emergency appointment, to have medical care delayed until the office assistant could reach me via phone for permission. I will never be able to erase the helplessness he felt in that moment, but at least now he never has to experience that situation again.

Since she was 2 years old, my husband has been a constant in her life. I remember the first time she called him daddy, which she did on her own and with no direction from me. It caught us both off guard and we just looked at one another in shock. My son, who was 12 years old, asked if he had to start calling him daddy too. I told him only if he wanted. He never did officially and only used the title "father" jokingly during Christmas or when he wanted something.

We figured out later why she started calling him daddy. One day the babysitter pulled me aside and said our daughter asked about the other kids who were being picked up by their dads. She would hear them call out "Daddy!" While we were still only dating, he began picking her up from daycare and she decided then that it meant he was her dad. She began calling that which wasn't as though it was. Glory!!! The girl was being prophetic and I didn't even realize it.

Six months after our first date, we were married. Not once, but twice. We were ceremoniously married on Valentine's Day, 2009 in Baltimore before an audience of family and friends. What no one knew at the time was I had become Mrs. Maceo Jones four days earlier, in the office of a Fairfax County Civil Marriage Celebrant where we exchanged rings in the presence of the officiant and one witness. Afterwards we went to Fuddruckers for an unceremonious reception. Maceo ordered his usual order of burger and fries; I didn't have much of an appetite. Although I was very much aware of what had just taken place, I was still in shock that it had happened so quickly. My first marriage, also a civil ceremony, was far more involved and required advanced planning, blood work and Department of Corrections clearances.

Exactly eight years and one month before, I sat in a D.C. courthouse waiting for the Department of Corrections' detainee transport bus to arrive from the jail so I could say, "I do." Waiting along with me were my mom, my godmother Barbara and the Thorne's daughter, Eva. I wore a short purple dress because he said he wanted to see skin. It was January and I almost froze to death riding the subway train in a summer dress. In my hair, I wore little white flowers and wrapped my shoulders with a sheer golden wrap. In my pocket, I carried the ring that I bought for him and hoped that he remembered to bring the ring I had purchased for myself, which I had slipped to him illegally during a visit. Extreme nervousness is mild compared to how I felt waiting for him to come out from the back of the courtroom. People came and went. People who arrived after me, were married and left before me but I sat there waiting and wondering if he was ever going to come out. An hour after my scheduled time to be joined in matrimony, a clerk approached me and my group with news I wasn't expecting to hear. "There's been a problem. Mr. Andrews wasn't on the bus. He wasn't ready so they left without him. You'll have to reschedule."

"What?!! No, I can't!" I responded. In my head the words were screams leaving my soul but from my lips they escaped as soft whispers. I couldn't believe it. How could he not be ready? How could he miss the bus, the only bus from jail? What else could have been more important than marrying me? As I sat trying to process how I got to this place, left at the altar, figuratively, by a man, with nothing to his name, incarcerated and facing life in prison? I couldn't look anyone in the face. They believed in this relationship because I needed them to believe in it. I was convinced his love would be what I needed regardless of what it would take from me, or how it would change me in ways that bring me down rather than lift me higher.

Seeing how deeply I mourned for what seemed lost, the clerk hesitated, and then said, "Or you can sit and wait to see if he shows up."

I looked up and although it was only pity that filled the clerk's eyes, I saw hope. "Yes, please. I want to wait." And with that he turned and walked away.

I can only imagine how those waiting with me felt at that moment. Most likely the same way I felt, like he was never going to come out from the back of the courtroom. But no one said a word. Although hurried activity was going on around me, I saw nothing and heard nothing. The room was silent and yet full of commotion. My attention stayed fixed on the wooden door to the back of the room. Each time it opened to let a detainee and court marshals cross its threshold, I held my breath and each time it wasn't him, I exhaled more deflated.

There were a few times that I almost said, "Let's go" and each time I was filled with fear of walking away. What would I tell people? How would I explain why we didn't get married? So, I sat and waited, not because I believed in our love to that degree but because I doubted my own self-worth and resilience more. Eventually he did come through the side door at the back of the courtroom and we were married just as I wanted. God had given me a way of escape, just like He said He would. But I didn't take it. I didn't know enough about captivity to realize I was a prisoner of my own pain and bound by the issues of my past.

Fast forward to February 10, 2009 with a brand new me and a brand new marriage. I'm sure sitting across from my new husband, who undoubtedly enjoyed his double deluxe cheeseburger, was not the time to reminisce about the failed relationship of years ago. But I wasn't reminiscing of lost opportunity; instead, I sat astounded over how God had given me a brand new day as well, without any of the drama. When I left the program, I knew emphatically, and probably would have bet an offspring, that I would never be able to get married again legally. In fact, that's why I didn't accept the proposal I had received two years prior.

God was orchestrating things and I was a willing follower. Everything I had done after giving my heart back to God seemed as if it was all coming together like a picture puzzle. Many pieces all separated doesn't make any sense, but once the corners are placed and pieces begin to fit together, the picture begins to form. Excitement sets in and you begin to move faster and faster because you can finally see what the end result is going to be.

I sat at the table in the restaurant speechless that I was married, and married to a man who not only accepted my unbelievably crazed story about voodoo rituals and witness protection, but who was willing to take on a woman with two kids, educated to become an architect but working as an entry-level administrative assistant, while not once ever making me feel like I should be pitied. He married me because he loved me and loved the way I loved him. He simply wanted better for me and for my kids. But that doesn't mean we didn't have adversities along the way. You see, just because someone loved me with a pureness of heart didn't mean the issues I had before we met all went away. My issues packed their bags once again and came along for the journey.

NEVERTHELESS

We both came into the marriage with our own preconceived notions and expectations of what marriage would entail. I came into our marriage carrying anxieties and flawed perceptions of love from my childhood. Maceo came in expecting to be able to keep living the life as he had as a single man. He thought he would have his life and I would have my life, and that my life included the bills, kids, cooking, cleaning, budgeting, worrying, planning, etc. Before our relationship, his life consisted of working 20 hour days, 7 days a week, splurging on material things and being cynical toward anything and everything "family". He was one of those managers who frowned upon employees' leave requests for family obligations only to end up as one of those people taking off from work for the same obligations.

We were ill-prepared for marriage, ignorant of what our roles were, and incomplete in giving fully to our union. We weren't on the same page and I would go even further and say we were in different books with different language translations, and one was a Kindle and the other a paperback. Sometimes I wonder where we would be today without Holy Spirit leading, comforting, and correcting us. But I stop myself from thinking about it for too long because I don't want to spend an excessive amount of time thinking negatively about my love.

He never hit me. He never cursed me. He never hurt me the way my first husband did but at the same time the pain was greater. It was like a spiritual pain because I knew the love my husband and I had for one another came with the potential to become exactly what God wanted for us. The life God had designed for us, we were at risk of throwing it all away. I felt so out of control and yet, I tried with all my physical might to control our relationship, or more accurately, him. I had to learn to let go. I had to really learn to trust God with this too. I had trusted God to bring him to my kids and to me, but now I had to trust God to make us into who we needed to be. I tell people who are considering marriage the importance of marriage counseling simply because of what we endured. I tell them, you will go to counseling. It's just a matter of time. If not before you say "I do", then you'll definitely go after.

By the time we sought marriage counseling through our church, we were at the point of strongly considering separation. It was important to me that we pursued Bible-based counseling. I wanted the advice we received to be in line with the same saving Grace that sustained me everyday. How can a Word be capable of saving my soul and renewing my spirit and not be capable of transforming my marriage? But there was another reason, one less righteous. I saw myself as someone who was "in the Word" and my husband as someone who wasn't. I went into counseling assuming the entire sessions would be about what he was doing wrong and how he had to change. My expectation was he would be checked and have to repent for not operating in a head provider/spiritual leader role for our family. Turns out, God had other plans for who would be checked.

Pastor Kevin Adams, who was a pastor at my church, was assigned as our counselor. I'd seen him around but I didn't really know him and had never heard him preach. Maceo expected to be counseled by Pastor Mike himself so when he saw it was Pastor Kevin instead, he was instantly uninterested. Maceo and I traveled in separate cars to our first counseling session. I had been anxiously awaiting this meeting. I arrived with my Bible, pen and note paper. Ready to take documentation of everything that would be said to my husband in reproof. Maceo arrived empty handed. And just as I had hoped, Pastor Kevin addressed him for coming unprepared. I was prepared. Just as I began to get puffed up with pride, Pastor Kevin turned to me and asked, "Did you suggest to him that he bring a notebook?" My smile vanished. *What?!* I thought. *So, I'm going to get in trouble for what he doesn't do?*

"Um...no."

"Do you have paper you can give him?"

"Yes."

"What about a pen?"

"Yes."

"Good. Give it to him and let's begin."

After that first meeting, I too was no longer interested in being counseled. But God had other plans. From day one, Pastor Kevin showed me that I must continue to honor my role as a helpmate. I am supposed to be someone in which my husband has full confidence, and who will bring him good rather than harm regardless of how he's behaving. He showed me that my struggle wasn't with my husband, it was with my faith. I wasn't a control freak as I'd believed all my adult life. He showed me I was actually someone who wanted to relinquish all control but only to someone who was strong enough and honorable to receive it. But first, I had to lean not to my own ability but on my faith in God to keep me. My faith wasn't going to my husband and I already had years of proof that faith in myself would get me nowhere. I had to live by faith, by **MY** faith, in God through Christ. I learned during that entire process that if I do what I'm supposed to do, if I operate in order, then I have the right to rely on God to take care of the rest. Even when it appeared as if my husband was out of control and out of order, I have an obligation and responsibility to remain in order. I must honor him because I honor God. My relationship is with God and because God had given me to this man, to whom I was now joined, we are in this relationship together as one. To hurt him or do anything against him, the man God has given me, would be like I'm doing it against God.

My prayer went from asking God to 'change my husband', to 'change my marriage', to finally 'take away anything in me that isn't pleasing for my husband'. Instead of coming into the marriage with likes and dislikes, I prayed that God only allow me to like what my husband likes. I know this may sound strange or crazy compared to what the world would have women believe; to be independent, you must never compromise no matter what. But when you go into a relationship closed off to giving, then you actually miss out on the possibility of experiencing more. I'm okay with sounding crazy to the world. Crazy to the world but honorable to God is fine with me.

When I changed, my marriage changed. I began to see him differently which caused me to be more loving toward him, and equally he began to see me as someone less judgmental and more accepting. I stopped comparing the things he did or didn't do against the things I was accustomed to receiving. One of the best pieces of advice Pastor Kevin gave me was to stop trying to save situations that weren't really in need of saving. I used the scenario of the two of us being on a plane piloted by my husband. I said, "If the plane is going down, should I not jump in and save it?!" His answer, "Yes, if you're on a plane." Then he went on to say, "But not every moment in your marriage is a plane falling from the sky."

He showed me how, although I claimed to want him to be the head of the house, I was failing to rely on him as such. I was constantly leaning to my own resources and ability to manage our life together rather than relying on my husband. God is obligated to our faith and obedience. But when we try to manage situations on our own, we turn our back to God's outstretched hand much like a toddler having a tantrum when mom or dad says it's time to go.

We were never allowed to blame one another. We were required to be accountable for our own actions and exercise of faith. Pastor Kevin's ability to help us see that God has already placed in us what we needed to make our marriage what God intended it to be. We possessed the power to change our situation. We possessed the authority to declare the victory in our relationship. Until we operated in both the power and the authority, we would succumb to the enemy's defeat. For the sake of our family, our future, and the ministry of marriage, we made the conscious decision to fight for what God has for us. From our obedience, healing manifested in our marriage. Affection became pure and more meaningful. We were intentional in our desire for one another, not just physically but emotionally and spiritually. I began to feel in my spirit his love for me, and yet I was strong enough not to rely on it. He didn't validate me and I no longer tried to control him. We simply love, respect and desire one another. This is the most wonderful gift I could have received, wrapped in the most wonderful and handsome 6 foot 4 inch tall gift from God, walking this earth. Boy, oh boy...I love that man.

Okay, now, back to the adoption. The day was surreal. I had gotten a text that my godmother Barbara would not be able to come up from Richmond, which meant we would be going alone. Receiving the news that she couldn't make it on the morning of opened the door to anxieties that I believed were long gone. Following anxiety were disappointment and dejection. The enemy is a formidable foe, one with perfidious tactics to weaken our faith and assurance that the peace of God is ours.

NEVERTHELESS

Knowing abandonment and loneliness were areas of weakness for me in the past, the enemy attempted to convince me that I was alone. It would only be Maceo, me and our two girls present as we solidified our family legally, once and for all. Immediately I had to adjust my thinking, cast my cares upon God in full assurance that even in this situation, I am strengthened and settled. Always seeking someone to devour, the enemy searches for opportunities big and small to establish doubt, knowing if we begin to think on those things that they will manifest in our lives. Instead, we must think on the things that are true, honest, and pure to attain God's peace.

Up to that point in the pursuit of adoption, we had not received any paperwork, notice of court proceedings or anything from our attorney that confirmed our hearing for that day; we were simply instructed by our attorney to show up on this day and time. We had no idea what courtroom to report to or any idea of what to expect. Just days before, I was in San Francisco, CA serving as a chaperone and mentor to the girls of the Prince George's County Department of Parks and Recreation's Team SMAK. The girls were granted a trip to witness and be a part of the Technovation Challenge Pitch Day ceremony. I left the conference a day early, placing my trust that adoption day would go as planned. This decision was a demonstration of my faith in action.

We were required to look beyond how we felt about the lack of information and put our faith in God that this would work for our good. We had to place assured reliance on God to orchestrate the affairs of the day for the victory that we had already claimed. Years earlier, we had overcome contention in our marriage so that our family would blessed as a result. I had to fight the temptation to be frustrated that circumstances weren't going the way I thought they should. I had to fight the urge to want to lash out at our attorney for what seemed like lack of preparation. I could not walk in faith and fear, nor joy and rage at the same time.

On our way to the courthouse, I called our lawyer but her phone went straight to voicemail. While I could feel the stress rising and the blood flow speeding up the beat of my heart, I remembered from where my HELP comes. I began to pray. "Dear God, thank you for loving me and making this happen for my family. You know I didn't want to do this alone and I wish I had someone here to hold my hand." Before I could go any further, in my spirit I heard God say "There is. I am." With an overwhelming sense of peace, I knew at that moment we would be fine. I didn't know how, but I knew we would. Then, like every blood-bought, child of the Most-High God, with a self-appointed social media ministry, I posted to Facebook: "Prayed to God that I didn't want to do this alone, wanted someone here to hold my hand." His answer, "There is. I am."

We arrived at the courthouse early in hopes of finding our lawyer in the courthouse foyer waiting for us. She wasn't. We checked the monitors for mention of our names and corresponding docket information. There wasn't any. I asked the receptionist for direction and she told us to go upstairs to the second level "where they do adoptions". We proceeded up the spiral stairs to the second level and the first face I saw sitting in the waiting area was the face of my pastor, Dr. Mike Freeman. I turned and the second face I saw was his wife, Dr. Dee Dee. I froze and forgot for a second how my legs were supposed to operate, but as if operating by memory, my legs took me over to where my pastor was sitting. With my mouth wide open, tears welling up in my eyes and my hand outstretched toward him, I turned back to Maceo to see if he was seeing what I was seeing. This surely had to be a mirage I thought.

Almost the entire Freeman family was present. Dr. Dee Dee was standing near her mom, affectionately known as Mom Wooten. Pastor Mike was across from them playing with his grandkids whom he calls his grand-kisses. His newest son-in-law, Tim Bowman, Jr., was standing behind him. Pastor Mike's oldest daughter and her husband, Kevin, who were there to adopt their son, were sitting in the area near the doors of the courtroom where eventually we would all go for our individual hearing. When I finally reached Pastor Mike, almost simultaneously we both half-jokingly, half-seriously said, "What are you doing here?"

I told him we were there for an adoption and he said they were too. Then I told him of my prayer, how I wanted someone to be there with us to hold my hand, and how the Lord answered me with the words "There is. I am." Then I looked down and realized

NEVERTHELESS

Pastor Mike was in fact holding my hand. My lawyer eventually arrived and just when I couldn't imagine it would get any better, Pastor Mike asked her if he and his wife could accompany us inside the courtroom when it was our time to go before the judge. I wasn't expecting him to make such an offer but I am forever thankful he did. We weren't alone. Though I know God is with me always, in the natural it was just as Holy Spirit spoke to me. It was simply perfect; led by God and perfect.

While Maceo gave his testimony on the stand, Dr. Dee Dee held my hand as we listened to his every word. Pastor Mike was tending to my girls, who were playing on their iPads and not at all impressed with the proceedings. I leaned over to Dr. Dee Dee and told her of my daughter's dedication 9 years prior, when Pastor Mike stood before me and encouraged a scared and fragile mom of two that God still has control over my life. I told her how her husband's words meant the world to me then and still does today.

There was a wonderful overflow of blessings that day and if I had allowed my frustrations and fears to overtake me, I could have missed seeing the beauty that was made just for me. The girl who was broken, ashamed, and unsure was now certain and confident in her own skin. I have so much to be thankful for and yet I get emotional simply because I know the best is yet to come.

15

Have you ever experienced a wilderness moment? I'm not a camper or someone you'd find in the woods by any stretch of imagination. Whenever I watch a nature show on television or read about the fun camping trips of scout troops, then I get the desire to go camping! But the desire doesn't last because I begin to think about how dark it can be in the woods, all the many animals that live there from the smallest insect to the massive grizzly bears, and immediately the comforts of my home and putting up a tent in the living room seem far more appealing to me.

A wilderness moment is not like a fun camping trip. It's just the opposite. When I think of the wilderness, I envision an area with dense vegetation that makes it difficult to determine the direction you're traveling. Nowadays you can hire guides who are trained to take you through jungles and forests but the idea of being in an uninhabited area with "lions, tigers and bears – oh my!" (*The Wizard of Oz* - I couldn't resist) leaves me a little unsettled. While there are many who would do just fine in the woods, I, simply, am not one who wants to find out if I have what it takes.

Wilderness moments can include times of bewilderment, uncertainty and anxiousness. Times when I felt as if I was just existing, and I couldn't figure out why or what was my purpose, those were wilderness moments. Or when I was lost in sin such as lying, cheating, fornicating, and turning my back to God, those were definitely wilderness moments as well.

Studying the word wilderness gave me even more enlightenment. The dictionary defines wilderness as an area overgrown to the point of no discernable pathway, uncultivated or lacking human activity, wild

NEVERTHELESS

and a state of confusion. In the Bible, the use of the word is related to where it is found, either in the Old Testament or the New Testament. The most familiar Old Testament wilderness reference is when the Israelites wandered for 40 years on a journey that was only supposed to take 11 days. Even after making it to the Promise Land, they still failed to honor God as they should have and as a result were forced to endure even more hardships through exile.

In the New Testament, wilderness takes on a slightly new identity. In Greek, it is used to mean lonesome and solitary, along with uninhabited, but it was not referenced as a negative place or a place to avoid. John the Baptist is said to have spent the majority of his life in the wilderness, crying out about the coming of the Messiah (John 1:23). His devotion was true to the salvation that would be available to all who believed in Jesus Christ and he honored his role as a messenger for God, preparing the way for Jesus despite the opposition he received. John the Baptist was obviously where God wanted him to be and was doing what God called him to do. He was not having a wilderness moment because of anything he did or as the consequences of poor decisions. He was in the wilderness by assignment.

Jesus gives us another example of how a wilderness moment may not necessarily be the result of operating out of order with God. When *Jesus was led the Spirit into the wilderness to be tempted of the devil* (Matthew 4:1), He was exactly where He needed to be, or rather where we needed Him to be. His ability to remain sinless and the response He had to temptations serves as an example for us, making us more effective in our serving the Kingdom of God.

We all have had moments that seemed as if we were in a wilderness, when the way through was unclear or whether survival itself was uncertain. God's people, during the time of Ezekiel, felt they were being held accountable for the sins of their ancestors rather than their own. Have you ever felt this way? Have you ever felt you were being punished for the crimes and offenses of someone else or maybe that what you're going through is not your fault but the consequences of someone else's transgressions? I know I have.

NEVERTHELESS

Although I may have wanted to assign blame to others for what happened in my life, and this even includes Satan, the reality of every challenge or less than favorable situation is that I have a choice in how I react to it. Every action has a consequence and this even applies to sins committed by others. A child abused by an adult; a man who spends years of his life incarcerated after a wrongful conviction; or a wife infected with HIV by her husband who had an extramarital affair are examples of terrible wrongs where the innocent are forced to endure the consequences of acts made upon them.

It is easy to recognize who was wrong or who was at fault in these situations. But where to place the blame for a boy who becomes a man that acts aggressively hostile towards his parent for abuse he suffered and holds them responsible? Or who's the blame for the man who gives up all hope and takes his life because of a wrongful conviction? Equally, who should receive the blame for the woman whose heart turns cold toward God because she feels He failed to protect her from an abusive husband? Should the person take responsibility or should they act out with a "woe is me" freedom? It may seem harsh but as believers, we have to be able to see anything that excuses offense or permits resentment is contrary to the assignment that we have as Christ's disciples. We will be attacked. We will be persecuted. We will be afflicted and aggrieved. Reaching the place of manifested peace that comes from God does not mean living a life without discord or conflict. Realizing that God's promises of peace means being of good cheer knowing that Christ has overcome the world. It means trusting in Him for strength. It means relying on His Word that our labor is not in vain when we labor unto the Lord. It means forgiving the actions of others and not using them to justify walking in offense.

> *Beloved, do not think it strange concerning the fiery trial which is to try you, as though some strange things happened to you; but rejoice to the extent that you partake of Christ's sufferings, that we His glory is revealed, you may also be glad with exceeding joy.*
>
> 1 Peter 4:12-13

We live in a society where it is acceptable to blame others, to find fault and take offense with the actions, words and even beliefs of others. Christians are suing Christians, children are abusing their parents, and employers are spending millions of dollars trying to stay current with what terminology is politically correct when addressing gender, race, and religion. All of it has one thing in common – it's all a distraction from the love of God.

While we are fighting with one another or blaming others for the struggles in our lives, we are taking our eyes off God and His love, the only love that can cover us.

"For where envy and self-seeking exist, confusion and every evil thing are there."

James 3:16

Failing to take account of our actions and our reactions is what holds many back from seeing the fullness of God's peace in our lives. I remember wanting to blame my mother for the decisions I made as an adult. I remember wanting to blame my first husband for all that I had lost. But at some point, ownership has to fall with me with regards to whose direction I chose to follow. While there are circumstances that I will have to live with that were the result of decisions made by others, I have control over how I react to those circumstances. I can choose to either let consequences prevent me from being happy or I can be happy in spite of them. I choose peace in spite of the pain.

I could go through the rest of my life with *what if this* and *what if that*, but the time spent dwelling on what was and wasn't will cause me to miss out on the joys of today and the expectation of joy tomorrow. The Bible says each new day comes with new mercies so why live in the painful past of yesterday? Take from those moments the wisdom that is revealed to you, learn from it and use it to turn that wilderness moment into one that glorifies God.

Amid trials or situations outside the will of God for our lives, we have the option of either submitting to God's Word or submitting to the situation. The enemy tests us, and although God allows some tests to happen, it is important to hold on to the fact that it is God who sustains us. When it seems like you're facing or enduring a wilderness moment, initiate an "*Aha*" response by saying to yourself,

I AM REDEEMED! I AM RESTORED!

NEVERTHELESS

I AM PURPOSED!

And believe it! Set your mind on the things that are good and pleasing to God, allow him to direct your paths, and watch God use your situation to bless not only you but others as well, through you.

> *"If then you were raised with Christ, seek those things which are above, where Christ is, sitting at the right hand of God. Set your mind on things above, not on things on the earth."*
>
> Colossians 3:1-2

Be careful not to focus so deeply on the circumstances of our wilderness moments and risk turning those circumstances into idols before God. Defined as *an object of extreme worship; a false conception or false god*, idols are anything in our lives that we give prominence, importance, and priority to the point of dependence and worship. There are countless stories in the Bible that warn against worshipping idols and most think this only applies to the days of the Old Testament. However, today we spend just as much time focused on and making idols out of the same silver and gold, except today it's done electronically or on credit.

When working to earn financial wealth to maintain financial wealth without honoring God as the source of provision and promotion, then money itself has become an idol. When power takes priority over doing what is right, taking care of yourself or others, then promotion has become an idol.

Choosing not to forgive or deciding that forgiving someone for a wrong they've committed is impossible, makes unforgiveness an idol. The guilt and shame that I held onto from my assault became an idol of unforgiveness. Until I was willing to let go of shame and guilt over what happened to me, until I was able to say and believe in my heart that I forgive the man who assaulted me, I would never be able to move forward in the area of love the way God intends.

Then there's the favorite of the day: social media. When more time is spent on the Internet and social media than time spent with God, in His Word, in prayer and meditation, then those outlets have become idols. Every area of our lives should be inspected to make sure nothing has been placed before or above God in our lives. With everything connected through technology, it can be hard to get away from it. Churches stream their services and allow them for viewing later, which honestly has helped to lead many to the Body of Christ. Bibles are electronic and tithing can even be done conveniently online or via text message. But even with technology, we have control over the who, what, why and how much we engage with it. When we spend hours scrolling through the status updates of friends and fans, or find ourselves caught up in the tweet-retweet battles over something controversial, then we have to stop, take a step back and if necessary, disengage. I love the deactivate option of Facebook because it allows me to suspend my profile temporarily. I call it my Facebook-fast. I recognized this was a weakness for me. Having a weakness is not the problem. Choosing not to deal with a weakness is.

While I understand the importance of being connected to people, and it is a wonderful way to share with family and friends instantly, I know what are triggers of distraction for me. I am sensitive to managing those areas that could cause me to lose focus.

Social media has been both a blessing and a curse for some, just as money has been to other. Marriages have ended because of both. Couples are either joint profile and financial account holders or the exact opposite with separate or secret profiles and bank accounts. Insecurities and disputes are revealed through status updates and a spouse's value in the relationship is based on their financial contribution to the household. These may seem like valid arguments for the sin of social media and money, but in both cases, having access to either of them is not the problem, the love of them are. It is the idolizing of things above the things of God that cause them to become tools of destruction.

Gambling, drugs, fornication, and gossip, are easy to recognize as destructive idols but what about the ones we don't discuss? What about worrying over something to the point that it's all you do? What about thoughts of defeat, shame, and even anger? Those are common and normal, right? So common that we do them without even thinking about them. But God is so awesome that He tells us how to deal with these and anything else that comes against the knowledge of Him.

NEVERTHELESS

For the weapons of our warfare are not carnal but might in God for pulling down strongholds, casting down arguments and every high thing that exalts itself against the knowledge of God, bringing every thought into captivity to the obedience of Christ.

2 Corinthians 10:5

Do not make idols out of thoughts of defeat. Do not allow worry, fear, shame, or anger to become idols distracting you from the purpose and plan God has for your life. Although I know I am delivered, I have to make the daily decision to not go back. Deliverance is mine but I still must choose to walk in it.

"So I raised My hand in an oath to them in the wilderness, that I would not bring them into the land which I had given them, 'flowing with milk and honey,' the glory of all lands, because they despised My judgments and did walk in My statues, but profaned My Sabbaths; for their heart went after their idols. Nevertheless My eye spared them from destruction. I did not make an end of them in the wilderness."

Ezekiel 20:15-17

SHARONDA JONES

While meditating on the word nevertheless in Ezekiel 20:17, I felt the depth of God's love for His people and for me. I recalled times when I chose to do the opposite or go the way of my desires rather than obey the direction of Holy Spirit. I even remembered how I felt when I was angry with God for the abuse I suffered at the hands and actions of my first husband and even the consequences of my mom's decisions that affected my life. God said, "***Nevertheless***, I spared them in the wilderness." Even as the people of Israel endured the pains of being exiled because of their disobedience, God's faithfulness never waned. There were innocent children, wives, husbands, siblings who were condemned to the same fate, as well as ones who were faithful to God despite the circumstances they faced. Those who honored God through repentance were rewarded with redemption. Those who are obedient and faithful to His Word are rewarded with 'nevertheless'.

> *"Nevertheless My lovingkindness I will not utterly take from him, nor allow My faithfulness to fail."*
>
> Psalm 89:33

NEVERTHELESS

And it is that same commitment that you and I must submit to God, giving our own 'nevertheless' to God just as Christ did on the Cross.

> *And He said, "Abba, Father, all things are possible for You. Take this cup away from Me; nevertheless, not what I will, but what You will."*
>
> Mark 14:36

When the circumstances of life begin to try to weigh you down, turn to God and declare, 'NEVERTHELESS, I stand on the solid foundation of God's Word, for the Lord knows those who are His!" The world says you should be fearful, declare "NEVERTHELESS, for I know whose I am and from whom my strength comes!" Regardless of where you find yourself, rely on God's Word to keep you, knowing when you give Him control in your life, all things work for your good. Failing to do so can create chains of bondage, tying you to the very things that Christ took upon the Cross on your behalf. If it's our finances, we can become too focused on money. If it's a relationship, we can fall into depression should that relationship end. It doesn't matter what it is, it is better to focus on God even if it means changing how we do things or whom with.

For you and I, who are ambassadors for Jesus Christ, a wilderness holds no power. Instead, because we have the power and authority given to us as part of God's Grace, we are able to go into a barren wilderness and speak life to it. By fixing our eyes on Jesus, according to Hebrews 12:2, we can stand on perfected faith to endure and not grow weary.

Why then should a wilderness bother us when we can be like John the Baptist, whom Isaiah spoke of when he said:

"The voice of one crying in the wilderness; 'Prepare way of the Lord; make straight in the desert a highway for our God. Every valley shall be exalted and every mountain and hill brought low; the crooked places shall be made straight and the rough places smooth; the glory of the Lord shall be revealed and all flesh shall see it together; for the mouth of the Lord has spoken.'"

Isaiah 40:3-5

It is with wisdom and with understanding that we can say to any mountain "be thy removed", not

NEVERTHELESS

doubting in our heart but believing what we say will come to pass (Mark 11:23), the wilderness moments we experience will never be able to overwhelm us. Instead of a wilderness moment in our lives causing trepidation or fear, we can endure with the peace of God knowing that the wisdom of God, Jesus, is with us.

Fear not, my friend. You've got this.

My Squad

16

I am truly grateful. Thank you to each of you who has taken the time to read this book. It is a dream come true to finally put the words of my life on paper. Writing about the last 40 years has been quite an experience. I have had to stop numerous times just to give thanks to God for keeping me through it all. Although I lived it, it has been quite the journey to write about it, and then read over it repeatedly, from rough draft to this final version. God is so good, always was, IS and always will be.

My family and close friends have been amazing through this process and have given me a tremendous amount of encouragement to keep pressing onward. As someone who should have been canceled from any and all blessings, God still considered me worthy of love. I am amazed everyday by His love, grace and mercy. I am thankful that my mom planted those words in my spirit at such an early age, that goodness, which is really God's grace, and mercy shall follow me all the days of my life because they really have. I can depend on His Grace. I can depend on His mercy. I can depend on His hand to keep me and return me back to Him, as long as I am open to His correction and guidance.

In putting this book together, I had trouble deciding how it would go together or how I would even begin. I didn't know if I wanted to be this honest, how much to include or even if anyone would want to read about my life. I started and stop so many times that I got on my own nerves. Eventually, I put it aside. I confided in a friend how frustrated I had become and that I had put the book idea on the shelf for a while. Her response was "It's okay. Just trust God." She said God was undoubtedly directing me and that I needed to take the time to hear from him. She was right.

Prayer Pause

Lord, thank you so much for the people you've placed in my life to love me. You are Jehovah-Jireh!!! Such an awesome provider! From those who have gone on to be with you to those whom I have yet to meet on this journey called life, I give you ALL the honor and praise for the love given and received.

Lord God, I love you and I ask for abundant, overflowing, bountiful blessings continue to flow in their lives in return for their love to me. I love them God, but I know my love doesn't compare to your love for them. I am just grateful for the moments that I have had to love them and be loved by them.

Amen.

Although I considered the book to be on hold, it was only on hold in the natural. God was allowing the words to come to me. God was still putting the words in my spirit that would manifest into the words you're now reading.

While on a break from writing, God gave me another direction. One day the motorcycle ministry I belong to, the Kingdom Knights, participated in a missions assignment in the neighborhood of Barry Farm in Southeast D.C. It was a beautiful day to be out and on our bikes. Our group had participated in missions assignments before, but this was my first time in Barry Farm.

Growing up in D.C., I knew Barry Farm as a public housing development located in an area of D.C. that was plagued with violent crimes. But I learned during our visit that it is home to many hardworking families who are attempting to live above the impoverished display of their surroundings. Deemed low-income as most of the residents are on public assistance, the community has been discounted by politicians, business people, and even people in the same community. In part because of its reputation, the neighborhood has since been slated for

NEVERTHELESS

redevelopment and will one day include luxury and mixed-use housing, shopping and recreation. Only those current residents who are able to meet certain qualifications for housing will be allowed to return.

One would never guess the history behind this area just by looking at its current condition. In 1867, land was purchased by the Freedmen's Bureau, a U.S. government agency created to aid newly freed and former slaves, to create land and homeownership opportunities. Blacks moved from the slum areas of Georgetown to this side of town hoping for better. Now, down from 375 acres to only 24 acres in size, Barry Farm and the remaining Hillsdale community, as it was named in 1871, measures miscrably in acreage to its former days. Once completed, with the changes proposed for the site, it will be hard to imagine the heritage the area holds for the city and for African Americans.

When we finished our assignment, which was simply to engage the kids with games and fun activities during the community day event, we mounted our motorcycles and proceeded to head out. It was when I got to the corner, I looked at the sign that reads "Barry Farm Housing" and heard the voice of the Spirit of God say, "You're not done here."

I paused for a second, shook my head and said *"whatchu talkin bout Holy Spirit?"* Yes. That's how I talk to Him sometimes. Don't judge.

Needless to say, I was obedient. I called the director the next week and said, "Hi, my name is Sharonda and I believe I am supposed to help you. I'm not sure how, but I know I am." In our conversation, I shared my background in architecture and my prior role as a science, technology, engineering, and mathematics (S.T.E.M.) mentor with the Prince George's County Department of Parks and Recreation. I offered to create a similar program for the young girls of Barry Farm. She agreed and from there, with 'A' for art added, S.T.E.A.M. Power was born.

Volunteering with the young girls of Barry Farm, created an opportunity for God to show me that I still had more to give. He allowed me to see my ability in a size that I could handle yet He had so much more waiting for me. While I served, my heart was being stretched to receive and to give abundantly. He wasn't preparing me for greater but rather God was preparing me for *seeing* greater. By accepting Christ, we are perfect in Him. It is through faith that we have all that we need to do all that God has prepared us to do. It is our vision or perspective that has to change in order to bring it to pass. We will never know what God has for us if we fail to see ourselves capable to of possessing it.

God has already put in place and placed inside you everything you will need for this journey in life. Regardless of how things look today, regardless of the mistakes or even decisions you've made that may seem like there's no coming back from, God has given you the power and ability to be an overcomer, more than a conqueror and His promises are forever.

And let us not grow weary while doing good, for in due season we shall reap if we do not lose heart.

Galatians 6:9

I thought my mistakes had taken me out of line to receive what God had intended for me. The joy that I had given up on having, the happiness that the enemy told me it would be pointless to hope for, and the peace that I thought was never going to be available to me, I got it back. God is a restoring God. He deserves our praises and everlasting love. We must be like David and praise God for His wondrous works, for His strength and for giving us the desires of our hearts. But this would not have come without first submitting all to Him.

> *"But seek first the kingdom of God and His righteousness, and all these things shall be added to you."*
>
> Matthew 6:33
>
> *"But from there you will seek the Lord your God, and you will find Him if you seek Him with all your heart and with all your soul."*
>
> Deuteronomy 4:29

Realizing that if my heart was fixed on pleasing God, seeking God, then the desires of my heart must come from Him. I used to think it was the other way around. I wanted to have desires in my heart, then seek God, believing that if I went to Him with desires in place, then He would bring them to pass. I know I am not the only person who believed this. But that's how the enemy gets us to stray into doubt, on a technicality. My heart's desire was to help children. This was a desire that God put into my heart. Therefore, this is a desire that God would bring to pass through and by my obedience. If the reverse were true, then my prior heart's desire to win the mega millions lottery would have long ago been a reality.

> *Trust in the Lord with all your heart, and lean not on your own understanding; In all your ways acknowledge Him, and He shall direct your paths.*
>
> Proverbs 3:5-6

With all my detours and paths rerouted, I began to believe that I had nothing to offer anyone. How could I mentor a child when I saw myself as a failure? What had I accomplished? How could my life be used to empower or inspire anyone else when I failed to accomplish my dreams and professional aspirations?

What I had to remind myself was that God can use anyone. The men Jesus chose to be his disciples were far from perfect. Simon, who actually joined the original witness protection program and got the new name Peter, had some less than Christlike moments.

James was known for being easy to anger and Thomas, well I'll just say many of us have had a Thomas moment of doubt. And yet Jesus held them in high regard enough to carry out His charge.

In developing my ear to hear from Holy Spirit, I learned to rely less on myself and more on His voice. I learned there's a freedom that comes from abandoning our own way for God's way. It's not a coincidence. It's not luck. It's not the universe or cosmic beings guiding us into an alternate realm of circumstances. It's first a choice to do it your way or God's way. Then secondly, it's experiencing the consequences of that choice. There's bad and good in life. There's trial and reward. There are situations in our control and situations that we have no control over because they've come from the hands and will of others. But the peace of God is a rest that no man can provide and no situation can surmount. Understanding that God has your back, your front and both sides means having the ability to face moments in life that come head on, and being unmovable in your belief that things will work out for your good. Which brings me to my first tandem skydiving jump, freefalling in the sky 10,000 feet above the earth. As if it was yesterday, I can still feel how exhilarating it was. It was something that I always wanted to do. My Godfather says he'll never understand why someone would jump "out of a perfectly good working airplane" but it's not for him to understand. I will never be able to explain and give justice to the experience. It's something that a person can only fully appreciate for themselves. The beauty of the tandem experience is that someone with more experience and equally dedicated to the success of the landing, is attached to your back. Knowing that person literally has your back provides the freedom to enjoy the moment. This is how God's rest is. Not that you're freefalling in life (even if it feels that way, know that God's plan for your life is purposed and ordered), but that you have the One who was in your yesterday, who is in your today, is also already in your tomorrow. God is on your side and His love is covering you.

After seeing the success of the STEAM Power Program at Barry Farm, I began to think about how many more young people are without access to similar science, technology, engineering, art and mathematics programs that also provide mentoring. God showed me a clear vision that my assignment didn't end with the girls of Barry Farm. It is bigger. He is bigger.

Shortly after the first STEAM Power program at Barry Farm, I started the Little Phoenixes Foundation to provide STEAM-based enrichment programs to at-risk youth living in high poverty communities. We are aspiring to offer post-secondary education scholarships to the young people who participate in those programs. Through Little Phoenixes, God is allowing me to experience something greater than I could have ever imagined. I am using my love of science and art, which caused me to pursue architecture many years ago, to help to guide and encourage future generations who are experiencing some of the same hardships that I once endured as a child. I am able to encourage them to look beyond circumstances that may include obstacles such as homelessness and low self-esteem, and inspire them to dream, believe, and rise.

God can use our "used to". What is it you used to do and have been delivered from that can be shared to free others from similar burdens? How can your testimony and "through-story" help to bring light to the darkness that may have others overwhelmed?

NEVERTHELESS

Don't allow fear to stop you. Don't allow shame to hold you back. If I said no to helping with a STEM program for girls in 2012, I would have missed the opportunity of being positioned to start STEAM Power or Little Phoenixes 4 years later.

Even with detour, after detour, I am as fulfilled, if not more, as I would have been if those detours never happened. By giving of myself to others, I am honoring my mission and purpose. I live to be a blessing and God is sustaining me in this life to do so. He has given us His Grace, which is the ability to do, be and have all that He has called us to do, be and have. If you have a song to sing, sing it. If you have a book to write, write it. If you have a spouse to love, love him or her. Do what is in your heart that brings joy to your life and glory to your Father in Heaven. A very special life was ransomed so that you could have joy, so why not have it? As long as you are operating in love, and God is at the center of all you do, nothing will be impossible for you to accomplish.

Be encouraged. Be restored. Be loosed from the shame, insecurities, doubt. Love yourself enough to let go of any fears that have held you back from realizing your dreams come true.

When you allow yourself to dream of greater, you hope for more. Combine your faith to believe it's available to you with the work to accomplish it and you'll rise in your purpose. Know that you are all that God says you are. Know that you are loved and that you were made from love to love.

Hold on to your faith in God to bring you through situations and circumstances that have caused you pain in the past. Rest in the assurance that you are more than a conqueror and an overcomer. You are redeemed and restored - nevertheless.

Prayer of Salvation

Have you accepted Jesus as Lord? Would you like to have His Saving Grace operate in your life? Then I invite you to pray this prayer:

Heavenly Father, in Jesus' Name, I repent of my sins. I ask you, Jesus, to come into my heart and be my Lord and Savior. By faith, I believe you died on my behalf and were raised from the dead so that I may be saved. I submit to your will and purpose for my life. Thank you, Lord, for saving me.

Amen.

If you prayed this prayer and believe in your heart, then you are SAVED! Begin studying the Word of God and join a Bible-teaching church to fellowship with those of like-minded faith.

Believe, by faith, to receive the manifested change in your life and you will see it happen.

SHARONDA JONES

Record the date here.

―――――――――――――――――

*On this day, I gave my life to
Jesus Christ and made Him
my Lord and Savior:*

―――――――――――――――――
―――――――――――――――――

ABOUT THE AUTHOR

Degreed in both architecture and engineering, Sharonda worked in the design/build industry for many years before switching her focus to empowering and inspiring others. She is the founder of Little Phoenixes Foundation, Inc., a faith-based non-profit organization to inspire youth to **DREAM, BELIEVE,** and **RISE.**

Sharonda is married to Maceo and together they are parents to Donaven, Maya, and Makiya. While she enjoys spending time with her family and the Little Phoenixes, Sharonda looks forward to moments when she can take a ride on her Victory motorcycle.

www.ingramcontent.com/pod-product-compliance
Lightning Source LLC
Chambersburg PA
CBHW020608300426
44113CB00007B/559